F O C U S   O N

Bidding

Master Point Press

22 Lower Village Gate

Toronto, ON

M5P 3L7

(416) 932-9766

www.pathcom.com/~raylee

Distributed in the USA by Barricade Books

50 Fifth Avenue, Suite 700

New York, NY 10011

1-800-59-BOOKS

Canadian Cataloguing In Publication Data

Roth, Danny, 1946-

Focus on Bidding

ISBN 1-894154-06-1

1. Contract Bridge — Bidding I. Title

GV1282.4.R67 1999   795.41'52   C98–932697-7

Cover and interior design: Zena Denchik

Editor: Ray Lee

Printed and bound in Canada

1 2 3 4 5 6 7   07 06 05 04 03 02 01 00 99

FOCUS ON

Bidding

DANNY ROTH

MASTER POINT PRESS

Foreword

This is not a book about systems, nor is it a book about conventions (although I confess I shall attempt to persuade you to adopt one or two in the course of it). This is a book about bidding, and about the places in the auction that we (and I use the word advisedly) go wrong. Let's take the opening chapter, as an example. I don't care whether you prefer to play a weak or a strong notrump, or eight-card majors, or the Purple Spotted Forcing Club. But I do care about how you decide when to bypass a major to bid one notrump, or what constitutes a decent opening bid and why, and what sequences you regard as forcing. You see what I mean about 'bidding' as opposed to 'system'? For the purpose of discussion, the example auctions are based on a fairly natural system with a strong notrump and five-card majors, but pretty well everything I talk about will apply, whatever you play.

Some words of warning

1) This book is not intended to be comprehensive; if you want an exhaustive treatment of something like negative doubles, balancing, or slam bidding, look elsewhere.

2) I'm going to point out some of the shortcomings of 'standard' methods in many areas, and suggest alternative treatments or conventions. This may disturb your peace of mind.

3) In some places I'm going to disagree strongly with accepted expert opinion. You probably won't go along with me at first, and perhaps never, but please keep an open mind and at least listen to my logic before you reject it.

4) Throughout, I'm going to ask you to think. A picture is worth a thousand words, and a bridge hand is worth any number of theoretical paragraphs. Stop each time you come to an example hand and try to decide on your own answer before continuing to read the discussion. Many of the examples are from hands I have myself (mis)bid and played, or are taken from expert-level competition. I hope I have learned something from them. I hope you will too.

Finally: *enjoy the book!*

Contents

Some opening remarks

If I may start with an apparent irrelevance: it is generally agreed among the tennis-playing fraternity that a tennis player is only as good as his *second* serve.

A parallel might be drawn with bridge: I am firmly convinced that a bridge player is only as good as his bidding! I have lost count of the number of players who are admired as 'top-class' — being quite capable of producing endplays and squeezes as well as brilliant opening leads and deceptive cards with almost boring regularity — yet, give them a simple hand to bid with you and you would be far safer on the *Hindenburg* or the *Titanic*. Attend any major tournament or read the daily bulletins, and rest assured, there will be plenty of examples.

It is said that 75% of all the points unnecessarily lost at the bridge table are thrown away during the bidding and most of the remainder while defending. This is probably a reasonable assumption; if anything, it's an understatement. In the bidding, you are looking at only thirteen cards, while during the play, you can see twice as many (and an increasing number as play progresses) and you have information from the auction to boot. A far higher standard of accuracy can now be expected and usually materializes.

Bidding has developed very considerably over the years. One only has to read match reports from the pre-war period, popularly known as the Culbertson era, to see how very modest the standard of play (in all three branches of the game) was in those days. Let it hastily be added that this is in no way a criticism of the players of that period. Just as, at that time, there was no color TV, space travel or computers, the game of bridge was still in its infancy, and by that stage had progressed that far and no further.

We now live in an era of very sophisticated constructive bidding systems, but as a counter, one in which preemptive bidding, particularly in the top-class game, has come very much to the fore. Fear of the accuracy of modern systems has led to a dramatic change of priorities. Nowadays, it would appear that the prime necessity is to make life difficult for your opponents, even at the expense of bidding your own hand properly. The prevailing rationale is that it is worth accepting the occasional massive loss for the more frequent benefits of the damage done to the opponents' auction. If you choose to adopt these methods, which include 10-12 notrump openings, weak two-bids, preempts and jump overcalls on pathetic five-card suits (S. J. Simon, who wrote the classic *Why You Lose at Bridge*, would be turning in his grave!), various types of raises that distinguish between preemptive and constructive and so on, that is fair enough. If you find yourself consistently successful with these methods, I shall not argue, although it has to be said that recent extensive research into bidding on sub-minimum values has revealed that it is unlikely to be a winning formula in the long run.

Here, therefore, it will be assumed that you prefer to bid constructively with less frequent preempts. There are enough opportunities to get into trouble, believe me. The purpose of this book, like its companion volumes, *Focus on Declarer Play* and *Focus on Defence*, is to try to point out some of the areas where players go wrong in the bidding. Some of these are the result of holes in the 'standard' bidding methods, and I'll make some suggestions about simple agreements that will help you and your partner bridge some of these gaps. For the most part, however, we shall be discussing everyday situations in which the rules you have learned are, at best, rough guidelines. You'll discover the right approach to thinking about the bidding so that when you do select a bid, you do it for the right reasons, and understand why your bid is the correct one.

Even the writers of fifty years ago agreed that it is better to play a bad system well than a good system badly. Make sure that, whatever you play, you and your partner are on the same wavelength. We're going to assume, for the purposes of this book, that you play a straightforward, 'standard' system, with relatively few gadgets or conventions. If you are familiar with the Standard American Yellow Card, you will be quite comfortable. This is a summary of our base system, to which we shall suggest modifications as the book progresses:

Opening bids

1NT	15-17 with Stayman and major-suit transfers
2NT	20-21 with Stayman and major-suit transfers
3NT	25-27
1 major	five-card suit, jump raises are limit, usually with four-card support; splinters; 2NT (Jacoby) shows a game raise or better, and usually four-card support
1 minor	may be a three-card suit; 1♦ will normally be four cards except 4432; balanced responding hands bid 1NT (8-10), 2NT (10-12, no four-card major), 3NT (13-15)
2♣	22 points or more or 9+ obvious playing tricks; game forcing except that 2♣ - 2♦ - 2NT (22-24) may be passed. A 2♦ response (negative) in principle denies an ace and a king or eight scattered points. Responder may use 2♦ as a waiting bid, intending to catch up later.
2♦/♥/♠	weak — a reasonable six-card suit with about 5-9 points.

Overcalls (vulnerability obviously is relevant throughout)

One-level: 8-16 points with a reasonable five-card suit
Two-level: at least a good five-card suit and opening values
Jump overcalls are preemptive, normally with a reasonable six-card suit
1NT overcall: 15-18 (12-14 balancing), Stayman and transfers still apply

Doubles

Negative up to 2♠
Responsive (after opener's suit has been supported) up to 4♦

Cuebids   Michaels (at least 5-5)

Slam bidding   Blackwood. Gerber directly over 1NT openings

Other   Unusual notrump; fourth suit forcing to game

By calling it a 'standard' system, of course, we distinguish it from one in which a two-level response to an opening bid (1♠-2♦, for example) is essentially game-forcing. However, it's worth a short digression to examine which of our bidding sequences we regard as 'forcing' (i.e. partner may not pass them) and which we don't.

First, there are several possible approaches when responder

bids a new suit at the two-level:

1) Only forcing for one round; responder can pass any rebid by opener.

W	N	E	S
			1♠
pass	2♣	pass	2♦
pass	?		

With this agreement, South's 2♦ is nonforcing — North has not promised another bid.

2) Forcing for one round, but responder can only pass after a simple rebid of opener's suit.

W	N	E	S
			1♠
pass	2♣	pass	2♠

Here South's 2♠ can be passed, but all other rebids except 2NT are forcing.

3) Forcing for one round but guaranteeing one more bid.

W	N	E	S
			1♠
pass	2♣	pass	2♠

Now, sequences like this cannot be passed. This allows opener to make a minimum rebid on quite a strong hand, in order to find out more about his partner's hand.

There are advantages and disadvantages of all three of these methods, and you'll have to make up your own mind which you prefer. However, the example serves to illustrate the point made earlier — it probably matters less what your agreements are, than that you actually *have* agreements with your partner. Allow me simply to offer a general tip stemming from the above discussion, then:

The more sequences you play as forcing, the less you will use them.

The modern style, which is to play an increasing number of sequences as forcing, lays the emphasis on big, primarily 'fitting' hands at the expense of smaller, misfitting hands. Certainly, a case can be made for this at teams, but even then, in my view, the argument carries insufficient weight. At pairs, there seems even less sense.

Let's consider a few examples. Remember that there is no 'right' or 'wrong' — but you have to have an agreement with your partner. In fact, you might want to go through the hands separately and see whether you both give the same answers!

Would you consider the last bid in each of these auctions to be forcing or not? In the first few, the opposition is silent:

W	N	E	S
			1♠
pass	2♥	pass	2♠
pass	3♥		

Many top pairs nowadays play this as forcing and they have a very good case in that this is the type of situation where there is likely to be a choice of game contracts, 3NT or four of either major. If 3♥ here is played as non-forcing, then a strong responder may have to invent a bid in a minor he does not hold if he is to force another bid from his partner. This can lead to insuperable preference problems. On the other hand, if you play this sequence as forcing, a weak responder has to pass 2♠, risking playing in a 5-1 fit or worse when a 6-2 fit or better is available in hearts. I think there is a good case for playing 3♥ as forcing at teams, where game considerations dominate, but non-forcing at pairs where it may be crucial to play in the best partscore. Talk it over with your partner.

W	N	E	S
			1♦
pass	1♥	pass	1♠

Many pairs play this change of suit as forcing, leaving the jump shift available for a mini-splinter or a fit-showing jump. This certainly has advantages but the problem arises in the likely event of responder's holding a singleton in the first suit and three cards only in the second, when he has no satisfactory bid. The raise of the second suit takes on a very wide range in terms of strength. I recommend that you treat this sequence as non-forcing.

W	N	E	S
			1NT
pass	2♣	pass	2♠
pass	3♦		

Here we have an auction where the opener has bid the 'wrong' major in response to Stayman and responder is something like 1-4-6-2. My general recommendation is to play all Stayman sequences as invitational but non-forcing (but there are many options available to you here, and we'll discuss some of them in Chapter 2).

W	N	E	S
			1♦
pass	1♥	pass	1NT
pass	3♦		

Here we are discussing whether 3NT or 5♦ is to be the final game contract. If this sequence is played as non-forcing, responder with a game-going hand has to jump in a new suit at the three-level to get more information, possibly misleading partner.

Now let's look at some situations where the opposition takes part in the bidding.

W	N	E	S
1♦	1♥	pass	2♣

Many pairs play a change of suit over an overcall as forcing by an unpassed hand; if so, South would certainly not be expecting North to pass.

W	N	E	S
1♦	1♥	pass	2♦
pass	2♥		

In this example, much depends on the meaning of the cuebid and how far it forces. If a new suit by South on the first round would have been forcing, the 2♦ bid would usually imply a limit raise in hearts while a direct 3♥ instead would be preemptive. If that is the case, North's 2♥ rebid shows little game interest, and South would need extra values to make another bid.

W	N	E	S
1♦	dbl	pass	1♥
pass	3♣		

After partner has responded to a take-out double, I like to play that the cuebid is the only forcing bid, forcing to suit agreement, notrump or game. Here North is probably very strong with something like 4-2-1-6, and is inviting game but can certainly be left in 3♣.

W	N	E	S
1♦	dbl	pass	2♦
pass	2♥		

Here we have had a cuebid in response to a takeout double. Some pairs play all cuebids as forcing to the same level at notrump, game, or suit agreement, i.e. usually guaranteeing another bid. I feel that this is unnecessary here. The doubler's partner is almost certainly offering a choice of majors and the doubler can always jump if he is strong.

W	N	E	S
	1♦	2♣	2♥

Here, of course, most players play the change of suit as forcing, ignoring the interference. 2♥ implies greater strength than a simple 1♥ response to 1♦ would have done, probably 10+ points, since the partnership is forced to a higher level even if opener is minimum. With a weaker hand, responder must pass or use a negative double if his hand is suitable.

This method is easy to remember, and it keeps the bidding low on strong hands. Against that, you cannot compete on weak hands with long heart suits, such as this one:

♠ 6 4   ♥ A Q 7 5 4 2   ♦ 8 6   ♣ 9 6 4

unless you distort some of the negative double auctions. Weak hands, naturally, are likely to occur more frequently than strong hands, and this is a drawback, particularly at pairs. Some partnerships play a change of suit as non-forcing (this is called a 'negative free bid') if the bid has been taken away (in the example above, the 1♥ response has been lost) but forcing otherwise, so that after a 1♥ overcall of partner's 1♦ opening, 1♠ would be forcing as usual.

I'm sure you can see pros and cons in all of these situations. The important thing is to have an agreement with your partner as to what the sequence means and to be on the same wavelength at all times.

Points to remember

1. To a great extent, it doesn't matter what system or conventions you decide to play; the main thing is that you and your partner have clear agreements on what you are playing.
2. Perhaps the most important thing to have agreed on is which sequences are forcing and which are not.
3. **Force breeds divorce.** My own inclination is to get your partner to agree to play as many sequences as possible to be non-forcing.

Uncontested Auctions

1

The first salvo

(the importance of the goal)

My first tip is that all bids, including passes, doubles and redoubles must be made with one consideration above all others in mind:

What final contract is anticipated?

The number of ill-judged bids that could be eliminated if only players had this idea drummed into them, to my mind, outnumbers all other bidding mistakes put together. For this reason, it will be worth spending a considerable amount of space on and indeed, many subsequent tips will stem from it.

The opening bid

You're probably thinking that this section is going to be pretty short — after all, the rules for selecting your opening bid on a hand are fairly straightforward. We shall start with some examples of common situations where players continually go wrong. Most of the time, the method of scoring will make little difference but we shall assume, for the sake of argument, that it is matchpoints and we are sitting South with neither side vulnerable.

As dealer, you hold:

♠ A K 6 4   ♥ 9 6 4   ♦ 7 5   ♣ A K Q 2.

What do you bid?

The hand falls into the 15-17 balanced category, so it appears to be a routine 1NT opener. That's certainly what the 'rules' tell you. But I'm going to shock some of you by strongly advising against opening 1NT on this hand for 'final contract' or 'goal' reasons. Unless partner produces a four-card or longer spade suit, it is very likely that, if you get to game, the final contract will be 3NT. If you open 1NT, you will be declarer, the last thing you want. Partner will need stoppers in both the red suits and they may well be tenace-type holdings like AQ or Kx . In that case, it may be crucial to have him as declarer. Start with 1♣ , intending to rebid 1♠ over a red suit.

While I was writing this, I came across the following hand:

North
♠ A 9 7 5
♥ 8 6 5 3
♦ Q 7 4
♣ A Q

West
♠ Q J 10 3
♥ 10 9 7 2
♦ 6 5
♣ 10 9 7

East
♠ K 6
♥ J 4
♦ J 10 9 2
♣ K J 6 3 2

South
♠ 8 4 2
♥ A K Q
♦ A K 8 3
♣ 8 5 4

South opened 1NT; North responded a Stayman 2♣ and, on hearing 2♦ from South, went on to 3NT. West led the ♠Q and declarer won the first round for fear of a club switch. After three rounds of hearts, he exited in spades, eventually making the contract by endplaying East on the fourth round of diamonds. East did not double 2♣ for the lead, and on balance, I think he was right, as his club holding is poor and broken and a double in this position was more likely to help the opponents. However, had he done so, a club lead would have defeated the contract as long as East discarded a spade and not a diamond on the third round of hearts.

In my view though, it should never have come to this. Nothing would make me open or rebid notrump on this hand. Open 1♦ and raise a major so that the auction goes:

North	South
1♦	1♥
2♥	2NT
3NT	pass

and look at the difference. You are now in the correct contract and the near-certain club lead gives it to you immediately.

What would you open on:

$$♠ A 8 7 6 4 \quad ♥ — \quad ♦ K 7 4 3 \quad ♣ K 7 5 3$$

Ten points and a void — a six-loser hand and an opening bid to most people. Personally, I wouldn't dream of it. Clearly, if you do open, it will be 1♠ — but what will you rebid over 2♥? A straightforward 2♠ hardly describes the hand. If your methods allow 2NT, that, to my mind, is even worse. This hand is crying out for a trump contract — why suggest notrump? If you pass initially though, the stage is yours. Consider what could happen:

1) If partner is weak and it is your opponents' hand, they will probably run into poor splits — perhaps all in four suits. Let them bid their hands to the full, using their 'accurate' system! It is quite likely that you can conclude the auction with a crushing double.

2) If partner opens with 1♥, you will be glad you did not open. The hand is probably a disastrous misfit, and if partner subscribes to the dictum that 'opening bid plus opening bid equals game', you will almost certainly end up in an unmakable contract, possibly doubled for an enormous penalty.

3) If partner opens and actually bids one of your suits, you can now go wild, insisting on at least game and possibly slam. Note that partner is now in full possession of the facts — that you are short on points but rich in distribution. He is in a much better position to make an accurate decision on the final contract, and if the opponents now bid their hearts, it can only help you!

As a general comment, opening light in first and second seats is very fashionable nowadays. I can only feel sorry for the majority of players who persistently indulge in the practice. The fun they miss bidding strong passed hands on the second round is incalculable and I wouldn't give it up for anything. Of course, in third seat, when partner has already passed, there is more justification for getting in on a weak hand with a good suit both to suggest a lead and to get in the opponents' way.

Here's another hand where the 'rules' don't work so well:

♠ K 8 7 6 4   ♥ K 8 7 5 3 2   ♦ J   ♣ J

This is another six-loser hand with length in both majors. It may well produce a game or even a slam in either suit, but care is needed. First of all, if you do open, which suit will you choose? If you start with hearts and then bid spades, you are showing reversing values — the hand is nowhere near strong enough. Bidding spades first and then hearts, however, risks finishing in the wrong major. At the same time, you have little defense, and if partner starts doubling the opponents, you're not going to contribute much. You could, if system permits, open a weak 2♥, but even the most aggressive preemptors would agree that, except in third seat, this bid denies interest in the other major, a dreadful distortion of the truth.

Once again, start with a pass and you are in control. If opponents bid the minors, you can put in a Michaels cuebid and describe the hand nicely. If they bid a major, your hand is automatically devalued but you still have the option to bid the other if the auction demands. In the unlikely event of their bidding both majors, you will be glad you did not help them by opening. Again, note that if they declare, they will almost certainly run into some most unfavorable splits — why spoil your chance of a big penalty?

These two hands illustrate an important point. Losing trick count only applies in trump contracts where a clear (minimum eight-card) fit is found; otherwise it is a recipe for getting too high.

What would you open with this hand?

♠ A Q 5 3   ♥ J   ♦ K J 7 5   ♣ K Q 4 2

The generally accepted rule for three-suiters is to 'bid the suit below the singleton', but unfortunately, real life isn't that simple.

A singleton club is no problem — you open 1♦, and even over 2♣ you have a comfortable notrump rebid appropriate for your point count. Likewise, a singleton diamond presents no difficulty — you open 1♣ and rebid 1♥ over 1♦. In this auction, a bid of 1♠ now by partner should be treated as forcing for one round (as opposed to other fourth-suit forcing bids which are commonly played as game-forcing) because it can be a genuine suit, covering the case where you are 4-4-1-4.

With a singleton spade, you aren't allowed to open 1♥ playing five-card majors and there is another problem if the hand falls into the 15-17 point range; opening 1♣ and rebidding 1NT over 1♠ shows only about 12-14 points. I prefer opening 1♦ and rebidding 2♣ — admittedly implying a five-card diamond suit, but I would rather tell a lie in a minor than in a major. The danger of opening 1♦ lies in the possibility of partner's being 5-4 in spades and hearts; we might easily miss the 4-4 heart fit. The third possibility, which very few would consider, is to open 1♣ and rebid 2♣. Yes, this risks a silly club contract, but if there is a fit in any suit, it will never be missed. My actual choice on any particular hand depends on suit quality. It is probably preferable to imply a five-card holding in the better suit, so that partner is misled to a minimum degree.

With a singleton heart, as on the hand given above, you will open a minor and rebid 1♠ but the arguments are still going on about which minor to choose. I have no doubt that, unless your diamonds are very strong and clubs very weak, 1♣ is preferable. If you open 1♣ and partner is 4-4 in diamonds and hearts, you will not miss the diamond fit. If you open 1♦ and partner is 4-4 in clubs and hearts, you are likely to miss the club fit. A further point, missed by most people, is that 4-4-4-1 hands are very awkward offensively but excellent defensively. In this case, you want to give the opponents maximum chance to come in. With the hand above, if there is a good diamond suit sitting to your left, you will want to know about it before deciding the final contract. If you open 1♦, your left-hand opponent may not be strong enough to overcall 2♣ and warn you of a club stack, but over 1♣ they don't need as much to bid 1♦.

Some partnerships try to overcome these various problems by sacrificing the weak 2♦ bid and using 2♦ to show a three-suited hand instead. As originally introduced, the bid covered hands in the 17-24 points range but these days, it is quite common to play it with a range of 11-16. But in light of this discussion, note that 1998 World Par Champion, Michael Rosenberg, wrote recently that he believes that opening weak three-suiters *at all* is a losing tactic.

Points to remember

1. ***Don't abuse the loser!*** Using losing trick count to justify opening the bidding on weak distributional hands is poor tactics. An extreme example will illustrate.

   Here is a six-loser hand: ♠ J 10 9 8 7 6   ♥ J 10 9 8 7 6 5 ♦ — ♣ —

   and this is another: ♠ —   ♥ —   ♦ J 10 9 8 7 6 5   ♣ J 10 9 8 7 6

The total losing trick count of twelve between the two hands suggests that we can make a small slam! In fact, with the ace, king and queen of all four suits in opposition hands, 6NT is indeed cold... for the opponents! As has already been indicated, if you open light, you are virtually guaranteed to get too high if partner has a big hand with a misfit.

2. If you are going to mislead partner about the length of a suit, it is best to do it in a minor rather than a major. The goal is relevant here. Accuracy is needed when considering four of a major as your game contract, but minor-suit hands are commonly played in 3NT and the exact length of the suit may not be so important.

3. Three-suiters, especially 4441 hands, are often better on defense than on offense. Don't be frightened of passing initially with sub-minimum, distributional hands, and keeping the bidding low if you do decide to bid.

4. Guard the tenace from the menace! If it is likely that a notrump game will be reached, attach the utmost importance to protecting possible tenaces against the expected opening lead.

Responder's first bid

As South, you hold:

♠ A 8 6 5 3   ♥ Q J 6 4   ♦ 7   ♣ A Q 10

Partner opens 1♥ and East passes. There are a number of alternatives you can consider as your first response: 1♠, 2♣, 2NT (Jacoby), 4♦ (splinter) and 4♥. Clearly, the final contract will be in hearts at game level at least and you can go several different ways from here. Bidding 1♠, intending to raise hearts later, is the approach many would adopt, but one I most strongly advise against. If partner hears 1♠ and holds a singleton spade, the holding you are dreaming of, he will devalue his hand, the last thing you want him to do.

A direct 4♥ is certainly a practical bid but since it is customarily played as preemptive, partner will almost certainly pass. Yet he only has to have:

♠ 9   ♥ A K 10 5 3 2   ♦ A 8 5 3   ♣ K 3

a mere fourteen points, for the grand slam to be cold when he would never make a move over your preempt.

Another possibility is to splinter with 4♦, which is a reasonable description of the hand. But I prefer a direct Jacoby 2NT, conventionally agreeing hearts and requiring partner to show you any sin-

gletons he has. Now you can get excited if he shows spade shortness by bidding 3♠ and devalue your hand if he bids 3♣.
Furthermore, after 2NT, even if partner has no shortness, you will find
out his strength at a low level and still have the option to cuebid your
controls in spades and diamonds later if the situation demands.

The converse case on the same auction is:

♠ K 8 7 5 4   ♥ K Q 3 2   ♦ A 8   ♣ J 6

On this hand I suggest that you *should* bid 1♠. If partner has a singleton spade now, you *will* want him to devalue it, while the ace and
lower honors in that suit could be invaluable in a heart game or
slam. Remember again that, if opponents enter the auction, they
can only help you — give them room!

This next hand is also a problem when partner opens 1♥:

♠ A   ♥ A K J   ♦ 7 6 5 4 3 2   ♣ A 3 2

You will likely finish in a game or slam in hearts and the question
is how to decide which. 2NT is possible but you only have three
trumps, and they're not trumps you are going to want to use to ruff
spades with unless partner's hearts are exceptional. On the other
hand, 2♦ is the worst bid you can make. The last thing you will
want partner to do is to devalue a diamond shortness, the feature for
which you are praying! Even 2♣ is not ideal; you do not want partner to devalue a singleton club either! A splinter 3♠ is a possibility
but splintering into a singleton ace also has disadvantages. Give
partner ♠KQx, a holding that would be useful for discarding club
losers, and nothing will turn him off more than a splinter in the suit.

So which is it to be? Of the options available, I might go for 2♣.
Partner is unlikely to have a singleton club and there are two added
bonuses. Firstly, partner has maximum room to describe his hand.
Secondly, and possibly more importantly, so have the opponents! An
overcall in spades, showing values there, would be a dream come
true. A diamond overcall is similarly welcome — if partner is very
short, he will delightedly upgrade his hand while, if he has an embarrassing ♦Qx, your partnership will be well warned!

To bid or not to bid your major on a flat hand? This is one that
vexes many players:

♠ Q 10 7 6   ♥ K J 6   ♦ K 5 4   ♣ A 5 2

Over a 1♦ opening from partner, 'practical' bidders will simply bid
3NT, giving away as little information to opponents as possible, and

this is certainly a justifiable approach. A 3NT response should always show a flat 4333 hand so that a distributional opener can confidently remove to a better game or look for a slam if appropriate. I am in favor of this policy when partner has opened with a minor and I have no major suit. Otherwise, as here, I prefer to look around. Remember, you can always play in 3NT. Partner could be 4-3-5-1, in which case 3NT could be going down on a club lead while anything up to a slam could be on in either spades or diamonds. Furthermore, if partner has ♣Qx, 3NT may only be making from his side. My choice is to bid 1♠ over 1♦; you still have all the options after hearing partner's rebid.

Here's another situation where the 'obvious' bid isn't necessarily right:

North	South
1♥	?

♠ A K Q J 7 3 2 ♥ — ♦ 9 5 2 ♣ 6 4 2

Many players would jump right to 4♠, the obvious final contract. But why? Whereas, if you were opener, this could be a hand with no defense against anything, after this auction you have massive prospects if the opponents venture in. With ten points in your hand and a minimum of eleven in partner's, you are assured of the balance of the high cards, while your void in partner's suit assures plenty of defensive tricks. A quiet 1♠ is all that is needed. Partner will then describe his hand further and you will probably sign off in 4♠ next time. But suppose an opponent comes in, with 2♦, say; if partner raises spades, he could well have diamond shortness, and now you could easily bid a good slam on minimal values, partner perhaps producing:

♠ 10 9 7 ♥ A J 8 6 3 ♦ 6 ♣ A K 7 3

You might argue that with this hand, partner should move over 4♠. But can he be confident at the five-level when you could have:

♠ K Q J 6 5 3 2 ♥ 4 2 ♦ Q 5 ♣ 4 2

Points to remember

1. Kindness to opponents will often be repaid. This is very much an 'against the tide' tip in these days of obsessive and indiscriminate overcalling and preempting but never forget that the opponents' bidding can be an

invaluable aid, not only to your bidding but also in the play. Providing you have no fear of defending, giving them room to bid can only be to your benefit. Modern aggressive bidders will seldom let you down!

2. Do not rush into a decision on the final contract when there is no need to do so. I believe this to be a most important and very underrated tip. Far too many players choose their final contract without sufficient discussion with partner in situations when a more careful look would cost little or nothing. For example, all too often players sign off in game when it would cost nothing to hint at a slam below game. The argument that lengthy bidding sequences are liable to help opponents find the optimum lead and defense carries much less weight with me. In my experience, the vast majority of cases will see them find the correct line anyway and in many more, their choice will make little difference to the result.

3. When a fit is found at an early stage and it is clear that the discussion is on whether to play a partscore, a game or a slam in that denomination, make bids which will help partner upgrade or devalue his honors, lengths and shortages accurately. Conversely, avoid bids that have the opposite effect.

Opener's first rebid

With the opposition silent, you open 1♣ and partner responds 1♠. You now need to find a rebid on hands like:

        ♠ K 8 4   ♥ K 2   ♦ A Q 8   ♣ Q 9 6 5 2

and

        ♠ 5 4 2   ♥ A 7   ♦ A K 8   ♣ Q 9 6 5 2

Clearly, on both these hands you have a choice between 1NT and 2♠ (2♣ is not attractive on such a suit) and again, goal considerations must rule. If the partnership is heading for game, it is likely to be 3NT if partner has only a four-card spade suit or 4♠ if partner has five or more spades. In the 3NT cases, you will want to be declarer if you have a tenace position to protect and if you don't, you will want partner to be declarer. I would therefore bid 1NT on the first hand but prefer 2♠ on the second. After being raised, partner should not rebid his spades without a five-card suit unless he is happy to play opposite three small. Rebidding supported four-card suits is a very common error — if I have raised on a four-card support, I can always go back to spades.

Now try these examples for yourself on the same sequence:

	North	South
		1♣
	1♠	?

a) ♠ A 6 4   b) ♠ 8 7 3   c) ♠ Q 8 6   d) ♠ Q 7 4
   ♥ A 6   ♥ A 10   ♥ Q 7   ♥ Q J
   ♦ Q 7 5   ♦ K Q 7   ♦ K J 4   ♦ K 7 3
   ♣ A 10 8 6 2   ♣ K 9 6 5 2   ♣ A J 8 5 3   ♣ A Q 6 4 3

e) ♠ 8 6 5   f) ♠ 5 4 2   g) ♠ A 5 4   h) ♠ Q 9 8
   ♥ Q 3   ♥ 9 7   ♥ A J   ♥ 9 5
   ♦ K 3 2   ♦ A K 7   ♦ K 8 7   ♦ A J 5
   ♣ A K J 8 2   ♣ K Q J 4 2   ♣ Q 8 7 6 4   ♣ A Q 8 6 4

The acid test in each case here is the heart holding — does it need
to be protected for notrump? The answer is 'yes' in b) — covering
♥Jxx with partner — c), e) and g) — covering ♥10xx — but 'no' in
the others. Note that, in d), you want partner to be declarer if he has
♥Ax; you can never gain from the lead if you are declarer.

Here's an example of another thorny issue early in the auction.
You open 1♣ and partner responds 1♥. What is your rebid on:

♠ K 8 4 2   ♥ K 2   ♦ A J 8   ♣ Q 9 6 5

Well, do you like 1♠ here or do you dive straight for 1NT? A common practice is for opener only to show a major suit at the one-
level if his minor suit is at least four cards long. If he has only a
three-card minor, he rebids 1NT concealing any major suits for now.
Thus 1♣-1♦-1♥ or 1♣-1♥-1♠ would guarantee at least four clubs
while 1♣-1♦-1NT or 1♣-1♥-1NT would not deny four of an unbid
major and would be bid, for example, with three clubs and four
spades. The logic here is that responder should not be in any doubt
as to how to give preference. Pairs who bid this way use some
kind of checkback method over the 1NT rebid, enabling opener to
show his major or otherwise further describe his hand.

These methods use 2♣ as the checkback bid and it is thus lost
as a simple preference is opener's first suit was clubs. For this reason, some partnerships prefer to use the unbid minor, if available, as
the checkback bid ('New Minor Forcing'). Using this convention,
1♣-1♥-1NT-2♣ would be natural while 1♣-1♥-1NT-2♦ would be
checkback, seeking three-card heart support or a spade fit.

I have to say that I am not in favor of either treatment, and always show the major suit if I can, even after opening a short club or diamond. For one thing, partner may not be strong enough to move over the 1NT rebid and secondly, if there is any doubt about whether to give preference to the minor or bid 1NT, my policy is to bid 1NT, whether or not I have stoppers in the unbid suits. The partnership is only at the one-level, and particularly in the absence of an overcall (and both opponents have had a chance to bid), it is unlikely that a lot of tricks will be lost in any one suit.

Points to remember

1. When deciding whether to rebid notrump or to raise partner with three-card support, consider the suitability of your hand as declarer in a notrump contract. The quality of your trump support is of secondary importance to the decision.

2. Don't be afraid to show your majors at a low level, even with a balanced weak hand. As responder, tend to rebid notrump in these auctions unless you have strong support for partner's minor. 1NT will often be the right contract anyway.

Responder's second bid

We come now to responder's second bid, and again the mistakes are all there, waiting to be made. By this stage of the auction, responder will have a fairly good idea of opener's hand and may be in a position to judge the final contract immediately. Often though, further information needs to be sought. Too many players 'take decisions' when there is neither need nor hurry to do so and often the wrong contract results. This is particularly expensive at IMP scoring in the game and slam zones. We shall look at situations where:

    a) three suits have been bid;
    b) two suits have been bid, opener repeating his;
    c) two suits have been bid, opener having raised responder;
    d) one suit has been bid, one partner having bid notrump.

Three suits have been bid

Partner deals, the bidding goes 1♥-1♠-2♣ and you have to find a reply on:

♠ A K 6 5 4   ♥ 6 2   ♦ Q 8 5   ♣ J 4 2

(the 2♣ rebid is non-forcing — you can pass if you wish). This is the sort of everyday situation where partners are guaranteed to make my blood boil and it is well worthwhile spending some time on it.

'Good five-card suits should be rebid!', beginners and intermediate players (many of whom have been playing for decades) keep telling me. The spade suit here is perfectly respectable so it looks as though 2♠ is the obvious call. This is exactly what happened when this hand came up recently. I had nothing more to say as opener on a minimum hand with a singleton spade (I was 1-5 3 4) and justice was done when the spades split 5-2. The contract went down three — a hopeless matchpoint score when 2♥ and 2♣ were both close to making.

Perhaps, on ten points, you considered the hand worth 2NT. The first thing to realize is that, although the combined point-count could be up to twenty-seven or more, the chances are that this hand has very poor prospects. What has partner shown so far? Nine cards at least in hearts and clubs, and possibly more, which means that nine of your ten points are in the wrong place.

The next question is: 'How many spades has partner got?' and this leads me to a new tip, a vital one in my opinion and yet neglected by the vast majority:

Sniff the stiff!

In this kind of situation, where partner has shown at least nine cards in two suits and you have bid a long suit, be prepared for him to turn up with a singleton in yours. This kind of situation occurs daily and still responders happily carry on rebidding their suit, presenting their opponents with modest but unnecessary penalties that, over the years, add up significantly at any form of scoring.

On this auction, partner could easily be void of spades.   If he has three, he should, in my opinion, prefer a 2♠ raise to bidding 2♣, since his singleton diamond would suggest that 4♠ could be a reasonable goal. As a result, realistically the best you can expect is a doubleton spade and you are therefore at least as well off in 2♥ as 2♠. You should certainly bid 2♥ in preference to passing 2♣; game could still be on. If partner turns out to be 5-5 in hearts and clubs, that is unlucky but well against the odds, and even in that case, 2♥ hasn't failed yet. Also, he still has the chance to bid 3♣ over 2♥ on that hand.

The next hand presents different issues:

Partner	You
1♥	1♠
2♣	?

♠ A 10 7 3
♥ J 6
♦ A 8 7
♣ K Q 8 6

Here you have fourteen points, enough for 3NT, and that is what most would bid now. However, I think it is ill-advised.to bid it directly now. 3NT is the hot favorite to be the goal if game is on — but you will want it played from partner's side, particularly if his diamond holding is something like ♦Qx or ♦KJ, giving you a likely extra stopper. The best bid is therefore a fourth-suit, game-forcing 2♦. If partner bids notrump, let him play there; if he bids 2♥ or 2♠, correct to 3NT and partner can take it from there. 3NT is still possible, but 4♥ or 5♣ might prove preferable.

Partner	You
1♥	1♠
2♣	?

♠ Q 8 4 3 2
♥ A K 2
♦ A 8
♣ K 10 9

Here you are easily worth game, but perhaps a slam is possible. It costs nothing to find out more about partner's hand. The possibility that partner has a stiff spade could work in your favor! Instead of committing yourself to 4♥, try a fourth-suit forcing 2♦. Whatever he says, you now bid 4♥, effectively 'in a loud voice' — partner may be able to go on. It costs nothing.

Remember to credit partner with some intelligence too. Look at this example of a very common error, which is taken from 'top-level' competition.

North	South
	1♠
2♦	2♥
3NT	?

♠ A K 7 6 5
♥ Q 10 8 4 3
♦ Q 3
♣ 5

Sitting South, you are vulnerable and pick up the hand on the left. Do you bid again?

At the table, South went on to 4♥, losing three heart tricks and a club when North tabled:

♠ 8   ♥ 9 7   ♦ A K 10 9 6 5   ♣ K Q 9 8

3NT was, of course, easy. To my mind, South was completely at fault. If North had any doubt about the final contract, he could have bid a fourth-suit forcing 3♣, enabling South to rebid his hearts, if appropriate. South's heart suit was a poor one anyway and he had no reason to bid again over a direct 3NT.

Partner	You
1♥	1♠
2♣	?

♠ K Q J 10 9
♥ 9 7
♦ 8 6 2
♣ 10 8 5

In contrast to our first example, you must bid 2♠ here despite the likelihood that you are facing a stiff spade. In any other denomination, those spades may not take a single trick. As trumps, they are worth four tricks! In that respect, neither a bad split nor a void in partner's hand worries you.

Points to remember

1. **If partner doesn't want to know, don't put your hand on show!** Fourth-suit-forcing is used either where you are going to game but partner does not know the denomination or where there is a possible slam. If the fourth suit is not used, assume that partner is sufficiently informed to make a decision — don't answer questions that have not been asked!

2. **Be unselfish but not a doormat.** It pays to be unselfish but you should not take it to the extreme of shirking your responsibility. There are times when you have to insist on having your own way in the interests of the partnership. Notably where you have a long, good suit with no entry, your hand will be worthless unless that suit is trumps; therefore, tell your partner in no uncertain terms. If he still takes you out, it will be in the knowledge that this is the situation and any consequent poor result will be solely his responsibility.

Opener rebids his suit

This time, the bidding goes 1♥-1♠-2♥ and you have to find a reply on a hand like:

♠ A K 8 6 4   ♥ 7   ♦ J 6 3   ♣ 9 8 6 4

The first point here is that partner has guaranteed *six* hearts. With that in mind, this hand is a likely misfit — settle for the 6-1 'fit' and pass. Game is almost certainly out and it is unlikely that a better partscore will be found. Worst of all, if you persist with 2♠, partner with a spade void might feel obliged to bid 3♥ and the opponents may start doubling. Cut your losses. Notice too, that your spade holding will almost certainly provide two tricks for partner when hearts are trumps while there is no guarantee that something like ♥QJ109xx in partner's hand will provide any tricks at all with spades as trumps!

Partner	You
1♥	1♠
2♥	?

♠ Q J 8 7 3
♥ —
♦ K Q 7 2
♣ A 8 5 2

Many players would bid 2NT without much thought; some would even bid 3NT. *But how are you going to make it?* You have no help for partner's hearts and chances are that he has little for your suits. Even giving him fourteen points, you will be lucky to make eight tricks, never mind nine. Far better to ensure that hearts are trumps and therefore, potential tricks. Pass quickly and happily. You never know — aggressive opponents might feel they have been 'talked out of something' and balance! You will be ready with a double they will remember until Judgment Day!

This will be a convenient point to introduce a new tip, the importance of which I consider second only to the 'Goal'.

Travance in the bidding!

I do not know if the linguists will accept it, but I should like to introduce a new word into the language: 'travance', a coalescence of 'trance in advance'. It is well known that on defense, you should do your hesitating well in advance (for example, over whether to duck an ace) so that, when the time comes, you can play in even tempo, giving away as little as possible. What is not so well known is that this applies just as much in the bidding. In recent years, I have got into the habit of trying to predict awkward auctions *as soon as I pick up my cards*! I decide what to do in advance so that I can make my 'tough' bid happily and without hesitation, thus avoiding letting opponents know that my hand has posed a problem.

The last hand is a case in point. If partner opens a non-heart suit, you have no problem. But when he opened 1♥ and you responded 1♠, had you already decided what you were going to do with a rebid of 2♥? If you are ready to pass happily, opponents may think that you are minimum and happy in hearts, so that they could be cold for anything up to game in a minor. One word from them now and they could well be on the wrong end of 800 or more!

The most common example of the need for this is the 'gray area' notrump opening. You pick up a flat sixteen-count. Clearly you will open 1NT, but have you decided now what you are going to do if partner invites with 2NT? If you wait for it to happen and then start thinking, you will give away your precise point-count to the enemy. But bid confidently and the result could be crucial either way. Suppose you bid a confident game: opponents will likely credit you with a maximum seventeen and may take desperate measures when passive defense is required. Conversely, if you pass quickly, opponents may credit you with a minimum fifteen and defend 2NT passively when desperate measures were needed.

For the remainder of this book, awkward situations of this kind will be pointed out and you will see how vital it is to think ahead. Especially in competitive situations, you can put partner in the most embarrassing difficulties by thinking for a long time, notably if your final choice is a pass or double. Now, if your partner's action is not clear-cut, the director is likely to be called and you may have to accept an adjusted score. Even if the director rules in your favor, at best a lot of unnecessary unpleasantness may result. It does not have to happen.

Partner	**You**
1♥	1♠
2♥	?

♠ A Q 8 4 2
♥ K Q 2
♦ 5 2
♣ A 10 4

Here 4♥ seems the obvious final contract but it costs nothing to show a mild interest in a slam by bidding 3♣ first and then 4♥ over partner's reply. He need have no more than the right eleven-count —

　　　　♠Kx ♥Axxxxx ♦Axx ♣xx

for example for the slam to be odds-on and yet he will have little reason to go on over an immediate 4♥.

Partner	**You**
1♥	1♠
2♥	?

♠ K Q J 10 7
♥ 9
♦ Q J 10
♣ A 10 9 8

This is another misfit but, with your tremendous intermediates and self-supporting spade suit, the prospects are still bright. A direct 3NT is reasonable but it may be better to try 3♣ first; partner may have modest support for spades or a heart suit so good that 4♥ could be best. Give him a chance to offer an opinion.

The situation is a little different when partner has opened and then rebid a minor:

Partner	**You**
1♣	1♥
2♣	?

♠ A 8 7 5
♥ A 7 5 4 2
♦ Q 4 2
♣ 7

This is another situation where even good players continually go wrong. The hand is a near-certain write-off on a number of counts — your dislike of clubs, partner's failure to bid spades or support hearts and your very poor intermediates. Most people would bid 2NT (10-12 points, partner!) or, even worse, 2♠, a responder's reverse, forcing a further bid. The 10-12 point range for 2NT should, in my opinion, be 11-12, ten only being acceptable if you like partner's clubs and/or have good intermediates. I recommend a pass on this hand — and by the way, had you decided on this before responding with 1♥? Here the level is even lower than in the previous example and opponents will be most reluctant to sell out if you pass in tempo. Another crushing double awaits them!

Partner	**You**
1♣	1♥
2♣	?

♠ A K 3
♥ A 6 5 3
♦ 9 6
♣ A 10 9 7

This is another situation commonly misbid. With fifteen points, you clearly must insist on game — but where? Clearly the favorite is 3NT, but you will want it played from the other side if, as is likely, a diamond tenace needs to be protected. It is best to bid 2♠. With partner having denied four or more spades, this shows a feature rather than a suit and invites partner to bid notrump with a diamond stopper. If partner cannot help, you can always support the clubs later.

Partner	**You**
1♣	1♥
2♣	?

♠ J 10 7 3
♥ A 8 6 4
♦ A Q
♣ J 10 6

With this twelve-point hand, you have a comfortable 2NT rebid but I recommend 3NT. You have two aces and you can upgrade the two tens which are likely to be useful — the ♠10 helping the spade stopper and the ♣10 possibly helping to set up the long suit in dummy.

Partner	**You**
1♣	1♠
2♣	?

♠ Q 9 8 4 2
♥ 8 6
♦ K J 6 5 4
♣ 8

This is another situation where it pays to be selfish. It is unlikely that you can contribute much unless one of your suits is trumps and 2♦ stands out here. However, if (like most people) you play this as forcing, you have to pass 2♣. Over a forcing 2♦, partner will be in an awful mess with shapes like 1-4-2-6 and 1-4-3-5. The following hand was reported recently, exemplifying the dilemma perfectly as a player fell between two stools. With North-South vulnerable at IMP scoring, South held:

♠ A J 10 4   ♥ 10 9 7 5 3   ♦ J 8 6 5   ♣ —

North	South
1♣	1♥
2♣	?

What would you bid now? Playing a change of suit as forcing, South felt obliged to pass. But 2♣ proved a nightmare, when North had to declare it with:

♠ 6 2   ♥ K J   ♦ K Q 10 7   ♣ Q J 10 6 5

Meanwhile, by contrast, 2♦ would have been a pleasure. If South intends to pass 2♣, perhaps he should respond with 1♦, giving the partnership the best chance to find a fit, even at the expense of possibly missing a 5-3 heart fit. If he decides to bid 1♥, then, in my opinion, he should go through with it and bid 2♦ now.

Partner	You
1♣	1♠
2♣	?

♠ A J 6 4
♥ K 8 7
♦ Q 8
♣ A 8 6 4

This one is awkward and far more debatable in that you do not have a satisfactory bid. In this sequence, 2♥ is a suit, guaranteeing five spades, and it is suggested that it be played it as non-forcing for the reasons mentioned in the previous example. Remember partner can quite easily have four hearts. Whatever you bid, partner could be in great difficulty with a minimum hand and may feel obliged to bid 2NT with ♦Axx. If 3NT is to be the final contract, you want it played from your side because of your diamond holding, and I recommend that you screw up your courage and bid it outright.

Had you decided this *before* bidding 1♠? Even if partner cannot help in diamonds, you are not down yet; assuming defenders find a diamond lead, it could be from ♦AKxxx or they may only be able to take four tricks off the top. It is my long experience that it is more likely to be wrong *not* to bid 3NT on this kind of holding.

Points to remember

1. *Travance — trance in advance!* When you can reasonably anticipate a bidding decision point, or a bid or rebid by partner that will give you a problem, think about it well before the auction reaches that stage. Bidding in tempo gives away the least information to the opponents, and avoids putting partner under unnecessary pressure.

2. **Stay in the frying pan if the fire is likely to be hotter!** If you sense a serious misfit, it's often right to bail out early, rather than press on to a game with lots of high cards but few tricks. Give the opponents an opportunity to balance, and you may well collect a juicy penalty.

Opener has raised responder's suit

We now turn to a sequence where partner has opened with a minor and raises your major. In this example, the crucial difference from

Partner	You
1♦	1♠
2♠	?

♠ A 6 4 2
♥ 9 6
♦ A 8 7
♣ K Q 5 4

when the opening bid is 1♠ is that you, the spade bidder, have promised no more than four spades. With partner guaranteeing no more than three, 3NT comes into the picture as a possible final contract so now a three-level suit bid should tend to show values rather than be a help suit game try for spades.

On this hand, I would insist on game with thirteen points opposite an opener, but, if it is to be 3NT, partner will need to cover hearts and you will probably want the hand played from his side. Bidding 3♣ now shows partner where your points are and he can now choose between 3NT and 4♠. Note that 5♦ is also not out of the question.

Partner	You
1♦	1♠
2♠	?

♠ A Q 7 3
♥ A 6
♦ 8 6 5
♣ J 10 8 6

Here you can cover both unbid suits and 2NT limits your point-count while indicating only four spades. This is invitational, and partner can decide how to proceed from there.

Partner	You
1♦	1♠
2♠	?

♠ A K 10 8 4
♥ —
♦ A K 8
♣ 8 7 5 4 3

You now have a sensational two-suited fit and will end up at least in game. But there is no need to sign off at this stage: show your void with a jump to 4♥. Depending on partner's side-suit holdings, anything from 4♠ to 7♠ could be on. Partner will continue accordingly. Again, remember that you are still below game.

Partner	You
1♦	1♠
2♣	?

♠ A K J 6 4
♥ K 8 6
♦ 8 6 4
♣ 7 5

Here you are certainly worth a move towards game. A direct raise to 3♠ tells partner little and indeed some partnerships play this as preemptive, trying to silence the persistent balancers. A more descriptive bid is 3♥, showing partner where your values lie. If partner goes to 3NT, you can always correct to 4♠ if you wish, bearing in mind that the suit is only a 5-3 fit and the nine-trick game may be better. Note again — decide now, *before* bidding 3♥, what you're going to bid over 3NT.

Points to remember

1. It usually costs nothing to make a small move towards slam below the game level, in case partner can cooperate.

2. Always keep the goal in mind, even when partner raises your major. You may not yet have found a 4-4 fit, so 3NT may be the right spot. If it is, from which side should it be played?

One of you has bid notrump

Partner	You
1♠	1NT
2♠	?

♠ —
♥ K 6 5 4 2
♦ K 7 5 3
♣ Q 7 6 5

First, let's consider the bidding after a 1NT response (assumed to be played as non-forcing) to an opening major-suit bid. This is another situation in which less-experienced players continually cut their own throats. Two important points should be noted. Firstly, the auction guarantees six spades. With five and no second suit to bid (i.e. a 5-3-3-2 shape), partner should leave you in 1NT. Secondly, the rebid is a sign-off and should be respected as such. If there is a misfit, especially when you have not been doubled, you should stop bidding as soon as possible. On this hand, pass quickly and hope they balance.

Partner	You
1♠	1NT
2♠	?

♠ 4
♥ 8 5 2
♦ A 9 8
♣ Q 9 8 7 6 5

Here a similar mentality applies. You could be better in 3♣ but again do not announce to the world that there is a problem. Pass happily but consider moving to 3♣ if 2♠ is doubled for penalties.

Where partner opens a minor and rebids the suit, 3NT is the likely goal and bidding must be oriented towards it.

Partner	You
1♦	1NT
3♦	?

♠ 8 6 5
♥ 9 5 3
♦ K 7 5
♣ K Q 6 2

This time, partner should have at least fifteen points and six diamonds and you can think about game in 3NT. On this hand, however, particularly at pairs, I would pass. Partner will need to have good stoppers in both majors for you to have any chance at all, and even then, you will probably have to lose the lead to the ♣A to establish club tricks. Note too, you are going to be declarer, which given your major-suit holdings, is not desirable. Worse still, both of you have limited your hands and the opponents will not be scared to double if cards are lying badly. You can, of course, retreat to 4♦ but that will also probably be too high.

Partner	You
1♦	1NT
3♦	?

♠ K Q 8
♥ 6 5 4
♦ Q 7 6
♣ J 6 5 2

Here you are justified in looking for 3NT, and you should bid the suit you can stop — 3♠. Partner now has enough information to choose among 3NT, 4♦ and 5♦, all sign-offs.

Partner	You
1♦	1NT
3♦	?

♠ 6 5 4
♥ Q J 5
♦ A 9 8
♣ J 9 8 7

The same reasoning applies here; this time you bid 3♥.

Partner	You
1♦	1NT
3♦	?

♠ 9 7 4
♥ 9 8 5
♦ K 6 4
♣ A 9 8 6

This time, I recommend taking the plunge with 3NT outright. Despite being a point less than in the first example I discussed, the hand is worth a trick *more* in a race in that you have a club trick *without losing the lead.* Partner needs no more than ♦AQxxxx and the two major aces, fourteen points, for the game to be cold.

Points to remember

1. When partner rebids his own major over your 1NT response, he generally has six of them. However little support you have, it's usually right to pass at this point.

2. *Aces for races!* Aces are important in a notrump contract which is likely to be a race for establishing long-suit tricks. Without them, you need to be stronger in overall point-count to justify bidding 3NT. Note that the same consideration applies to defenders when they are considering doubling or competing. Actually, this illustrates a prime criticism of the standard point-count — ace 4, king 3, queen 2, jack 1. Taking the king as 'standard', the scale tends to significantly undervalue the ace while overvaluing the queen and the jack.

2

Running on the flat

After a notrump opening bid, on game-going hands your goal will normally be either 3NT or four of a major; the first question is how you get there. The basic bidding approach we started with includes Stayman and major-suit transfers. However, there are any number of popular conventions in use today that enable to you to improve on this structure; it's worth discussing the pros and cons of some of them in detail, and then making recommendations before we go on to look at more general bidding issues.

You are probably aware that the fundamental convention popularized by Sam Stayman has seen a lot of refinement over the years. It started off with the 2♣ response to a 1NT opening being a basic inquiry about four-card majors; partner responded 2♦ with no major, 2♥ with hearts alone or with both, and 2♠ with spades only. In modern times, there are a number of variants and extensions worthy of mention.

Two-way Stayman

This 'Blue Club'-style approach distinguishes between invitational and game-forcing hands. 2♣ is the 'weaker' variety, primarily designed to find the best part-score away from notrump or to stop in 2NT if opener is minimum in his range. 2♦ over 1NT is game-forcing, partner showing his major (or hearts with both), or a five-card minor, or responding 2NT without either. This has advantages in that the early game force gives the partnership more room to discuss slam possibilities below game. However, you give up the use of 2♦ as a transfer and you have to play 2♥ and 2♠ as natural weak takeouts. Not only are these contracts being played from the wrong side but you lose a round of constructive bidding with two-suited hands (one of the principal advantages of the transfer), and therefore I do not recommend this approach. It's more useful on very strong hands as opposed to the far more common weak ones.

Forcing Stayman

Here 2♣ has its usual meaning but is considered forcing at least as far as 2NT. Again, there is more room to discuss the big hands but the loss is considerable. With shapes like 5-4-2-2, 4-5-2-2, 4-4-4-1, 3-4-5-1 and 4-3-5-1 and few or no points, you cannot use Stayman to escape in a suit contract at the two-level. For me, this is too big a price to pay.

Slam-try Stayman

A variant of two-way Stayman where 2♦ shows slammish intentions and again allows low-level discussions below game. Opener is expected to answer as follows:

2♥	four-card heart suit only
2♠	four-card spade suit only
2NT	no major and minimum in the range
3♣	four cards in each major
3♦	no major but maximum in the range
3♥	five-card heart suit
3♠	five-card spade suit

Again, this sacrifices an important bid to deal with situations that are much rarer and I strongly advise against using it — it just isn't worthwhile.

Stopper Stayman

This is a variant of two-way Stayman in which 2♣ keeps its use to find major-suit fits while 2♦ is used to find out about stoppers in situations where a suit might be open in 3NT, with five of a minor being the only makable game. Opener is expected to bid a major suit in which his holding is Q10x or better, or 2NT if he has both major suits stopped. He bids three of his better minor if he has neither major stopped. Once again, the frequency of such hands is so low that I do not feel it is worth sacrificing the 2♦ bid and again, I do not recommend it.

Minor-suit Stayman (MSS)

This can be used by a partnership using simple major-suit transfers (2♦ for hearts and 2♥ for spades as discussed below) because now the 2♠ bid is idle. Bidding 2♠ shows slam interest, and asks opener to bid 3♣ with four or more clubs, 3♦ with four or more diamonds, and three of his stronger major with four cards in both minors. With no four-card minor, 2NT shows a maximum opener while 3NT, a quick move to game, shows a minimum. Note the departure from the normal meanings. In an auction where we are deciding at what level to play the hand, 2NT usually shows a minimum hand and can be passed while 3NT shows a maximum. Here the reverse applies; we are committed to game, so bidding it directly shows a minimum. This approach is known as 'The Principal of Fast Arrival' and will be discussed in more detail in the next chapter.

While MSS can be a useful gadget, minor-suit slams on 4-4 fits in otherwise balanced hands are very rare and I feel the 2♠ bid can be put to better use, as we shall see.

Five-card Stayman

This variant is much more useful over a 2NT opening, which can easily include a five-card major; however, it can also be used over 1NT. Over 2NT, 3♣ is the inquiry; opener shows his five-card major or bids 3♦ holding one or two four-card majors. He bids 3NT with no four-card major. After 3♦, responder can bid his major (or hearts with both) and a fit is found from there. Alternatively, some partnerships prefer to make the strong hand declarer — responder bids the major he does *not* hold. This is certainly an advantageous agreement, but be careful to remember it when it comes up!

Over 1NT, 3♦ is played as five-card Stayman (responder will

commonly have a small singleton about which he is worried in notrump); opener bids a five-card or very strong (prepared to play
opposite three small) four-card major or 3NT with no major. This
gives up the 3♦ invitational (long suit) bid and therefore, I do not
recommend it. It is also possible to play 2♣ as five-card Stayman, but
the sequences become very awkward, and you will almost certainly
lose your ability to invite game in notrump — a significant drawback.

Transfers

Whole books can and have been written about notrump bidding
structures that use transfers. Many partnerships confine themselves
to using 2♦ and 2♥ as major-suit transfers, leaving 2♠ available for
other purposes. For example, you could use 2♠ and 2NT for very
precise notrump raises — typically, opposite the standard 15-17
opener, 2♠ would be exactly eight points while 2NT would be nine.

We discussed using 2♠ as Minor-suit Stayman earlier in this
chapter, but a third possibility is to use 2♠ as an unspecified minor-
suit transfer, usually to be used on weak hands. Opener is expected
to bid 3♣ which will be passed or corrected to 3♦ as the final contract. 2NT is still a natural notrump raise, while 2♣ followed by
2NT guarantees at least one four-card major.

A fourth possibility, and the one I strongly recommend, is to
play four-suit transfers.

2♣	Stayman as usual but you must use it to get to a quantitative raise to 2NT and therefore this does not promise a four-card major.
2♦	Transfer to hearts.
2♥	Transfer to spades.
2♠	Transfer to clubs. Opener is expected to bid 3♣ with a poor club holding, but with three to an honor or better in clubs, he 'breaks' the transfer to 2NT, (often referred to as 'super-accepting') giving the responder the option of signing off in 3♣ or bidding on if he intended to offer 3NT as a con- tract or try for game or slam in the minor.
2NT	Transfer to diamonds; a similar treatment applies but, of course, the 'break' bid is 3♣.

This system solves all problems related to weak and strong hands
with a long minor suit, particularly when those including one four-
card major. With weak hands, you bid 2♣ and then, if partner bids

the 'wrong' major, you sign off in three of your minor. With strong hands, where you want to play at least in game and maybe in slam, you transfer to the minor and then bid the major, forcing to 3NT or four of the minor.

You can, if you wish, add four-level (Texas) major-suit transfers to this, or indeed, almost any structure. The combination of four-level and two-level transfers allows the introduction of some subtle shades of meaning, of which not everyone is aware. For example, since 1NT-4♦-4♥-pass is possible, then 1NT-2♦-2♥-4♥ is a mild slam try.   Similarly 1NT-2♦-2♥-4NT is quantitative, while 1NT-4♦-4♥-4NT is whatever flavor of Blackwood you are playing.

One problem sequence playing Stayman with 4-way transfers is the following:

You	Partner	
1♦	2♣	Your 2♥ bid does not deny spades, and your exact point-count is still undefined.
2♥	?	So is 2♠ forcing or not, and if not, what kind of hand does partner have?

The problem is actually easily solved — you can play it either way. Some partnerships play it as forcing, and initiating slam exploration. However, it makes much more sense to me to play it as non-forcing. Remember, 1NT-2NT is a transfer to diamonds, so the only way to invite game in notrump is to go through Stayman first. The result of this is that when the auction goes:

You	Partner
1NT	2♣
2♥	2NT

you cannot rely on partner's having four spades. However, if partner can bid 2♠ here with invitational values and a four-card spade suit, then 2NT must show invitational values and no four-card spade suit, and the difficulty vanishes.   There is one other advantage if 2♠ is played here as non-forcing, as will be seen shortly.

You	Partner	
1♦	2♣	Assuming then, that you have agreed to play 2♠ in this auction as non-forcing, opener either:
2♥	?	

1) with a four-card spade suit, passes or bids 3♠ according to his strength;
2) bids 2NT with no four-card spade suit and a minimum 1NT; or
3) bids 3♣ with no four-card spade suit and a maximum 1NT and now responder can pass, bid 3♦, or bid 3NT according to his hand.

This last rebid (3♣) allows responder to use this kind of sequence on a weak hand with a six-card minor and a four-card major. With this hand, having failed to find the major-suit landing spot, responder can pass 3♣ or correct to 3♦, which opener must pass. This option is another solid reason for playing the 2♠ rebid by responder as non-forcing.

For the remainder of this chapter, we shall assume that you have agreed to adopt this four-suit transfer structure at the two-level over a 1NT opening. Let's look at what bids at the three-level mean.

The usual method is to play 3♣ or 3♦ in response to a 1NT opening as a reasonable six-card or longer suit with two of the three top honors, invitational to 3NT but non-forcing. In practice, the point-count will be about 7-8. Opener is expected to bid 3NT if he can help with the long suit. Typically this means producing the outstanding honor or something like Jxxx, (which will prevent your being cut off from dummy), and good stoppers outside.

The major-suit bids, 3♥ and 3♠, can be played as preemptive — six-card or longer suits and about 0-3 points. They are also commonly played as slam tries, showing a good six-card suit or better, and requiring opener to cuebid. Neither comes up very often, so take your pick.

Points to remember

1. There are many possible structures you can play over a 1NT opening. Whatever you choose, you should be able to:
   a) Locate a 4-4 major-suit fit.
   b) Get out in a partscore on a weak hand.
   c) Invite partner to bid game in notrump or a major.
   d) Explore slam possibilities on strong distributional hands.

2. I recommend using Stayman with four-suit transfers as the most flexible system, but there are many other viable alternatives Just make sure that whatever structure you use covers everything listed in Point 1.

Where did we go wrong?

As the last chapter pointed out, the most common errors in notrump bidding are associated with players rushing into a final contract when there is no need to do so. An extra round of bidding and a further consultation with partner can often make the difference in regard to playing in the right contract, crucial at any form of scoring.

We shall start here, as we did our system discussion, with

Stayman. Remember, we have now agreed to play four-suit transfers.

You	Partner
1NT	2♣
2♥	2NT
?	

♠ A 9 7
♥ K Q 6 4
♦ A K J 5
♣ 9 6

With a maximum, we are likely to have enough for game but where do we want to play this hand? The obvious choice is 3NT but four of either major could actually be better on a 4-3 fit if partner is weak in clubs. To clarify the position, why not bid 3♦ now? Partner can then choose his action: 3NT, support your hearts or bid a good four-card spade-suit if he has one.

You	Partner
1NT	2♣
2♦	2NT
?	

♠ K Q 7
♥ 6 4
♦ A J 8 6
♣ A K 4 2

What about this example? Partner could have one or both majors; you have a maximum and are therefore entitled to bid again but why commit yourself to 3NT when 4♠ might be better? Bidding 3♠ is preferable here. Since you've denied a four-card major already, it will be clear to partner that you have three good spades and are worried about hearts, and he will choose the contract accordingly.

You	Partner
1NT	2♣
2♥	3♥
?	

♠ K Q 8
♥ A J 7 5
♦ 8 6 4
♣ A K 5

Again, you have a maximum and are entitled to bid on, but with a dead-flat hand, it is not clear whether game is safer in hearts or notrump. Sometimes the same nine tricks are available in both contracts! Once again, a no-cost 3♠ will make it clear to partner that you have worries in at least one of the minors and he can decide from there.

Turning our attention to transfers, suppose you open 1NT and partner bids 2♦, a transfer to 2♥. In my view, you should only be allowed to break the transfer with four trumps, in accordance with the Law of Total Tricks (we have at least nine trumps and so can justify bidding to the three-level). I recommend bidding:
    1) Three of partner's major with a minimum notrump opener.
    2) 2NT with a flat 3-4-3-3 maximum.

3) 2♠, 3♣ or 2♦ with a good suit and a maximum unbalanced hand; (some partnerships prefer to bid a poor doubleton or to bid 2NT if their doubleton is strong — there is nothing wrong with that; you just have to agree to do it).

So let's suppose that you bid a straightforward 2♥, and now partner bids 3♣. Any change of suit after a transfer is natural (at least four cards in principle, although there are exceptions on strong hands), forcing at least to three of the transferred major, here 3♥.

You	Partner
1NT	2♦
2♥	3♣
?	

♠ A K 7 5
♥ K 6
♦ 7 5 3
♣ A K 6 5

You have a maximum and therefore enough to insist on game, but the right contract could still be 3NT, 4♥ or 5♣ according to partner's length in his bid suits and his diamond quality. You can clarify this by bidding 3♠. Partner will recognize your diamond weakness and bid 3NT only if he is well stopped in that suit. On the other hand, he is well equipped to drive on even to a grand slam in clubs or hearts if he is void in diamonds! Let him take the decision on where to play.

You	Partner
1NT	2♦
2♥	3♣
?	

♠ 8 6 2
♥ A 6
♦ K Q 7 6
♣ A K 9 2

This is similar to the previous example and the same logic applies; this time you can bid 3♦ to show where your values are. This is forcing, and if he bids 3♥ (non-forcing and minimum), you can return to 4♣, which is only invitational as you have limited your hand.

You	Partner
1NT	2♦
2♥	3♣
?	

♠ K Q 3 2
♥ 8 5
♦ A J 3 2
♣ A J 7

This is a minimum hand with no real fit, and you must clarify this to partner by bidding 3♥. Note that this bid does not promise more than your minimum doubleton in the suit. Your very poor intermediates in the unbid suits suggest that 3NT will not be a success. It is now up to partner.

You	Partner
1NT	2♦
2♥	3♣
?	

♠ A 8 4 2
♥ K Q 9
♦ 8 4
♣ A K J 4

Here you have a maximum, and a good one at that, with every point where partner wants it. Do not be content with just bidding 4♥ —make an advance cuebid of 3♠ first. Initially, partner will take this as an invitation to 3NT, looking for a diamond stopper from him; however, when he bids 3NT you will remove to 4♥, effectively bidding the game 'in a loud voice.' Partner will move if his hand warrants it. It is, of course, tempting to bid 4♣ over 3♣, but, if partner is minimum, he might feel obliged to sign off in 5♣, missing the best game. Yes, there are situations where 6♣ will make while 6♥ will not, but your first priority must be to find the correct game contract.

There are common pitfalls for responder in transfer auctions, as well as for the opening bidder. The following are examples of sequences that contain snares for the unwary:

Partner	You
1NT	2♦
2♥	?

♠ 9 7 3
♥ A K Q J 10
♦ 7 5
♣ 7 6 5

You certainly have enough to bid a game, but the number of people who bid a 'straightforward' 4♥ in this situation ('because my hearts are so good, partner!') frightens me. Even ignoring the method of scoring, there is no guarantee that there is any benefit in having hearts as trumps and remember (again forgetting the matchpoint scoring consideration) playing there needs to have a *two-trick* advantage to be justified. You are considering the position where there are ten tricks in hearts but only eight in notrump. This is for partner to decide, primarily by considering his ruffing potential. Just bid 3NT showing the 3-5-3-2 shape, and accept his decision.

Partner	You
1NT	2♥
2♠	?

♠ A Q 9 7 4
♥ K 4
♦ 8 6 4 2
♣ Q 7

Again you have enough for game, but this time you have a second suit should you bid it, weak as it is? I suggest not in this case. It is highly unlikely that the only makable game is 5♦ and you should not imply the possibility. If you bid 3♦, partner will think that he is expected to produce stoppers in clubs and hearts and may be misled. A direct 3NT is better, offering a choice between that contract or 4♠.

Partner	You
1NT	2♥
2♠	?

♠ K Q 8 7 4 3
♥ 8 5
♦ A K Q
♣ 7 5

Yes, 4♠ should be comfortable but a slam could easily be on. It costs nothing to bid 3♦ first, intending to correct to 4♠ over 3♠ or 3NT. There is little danger of partner's bidding 4♦. Openers should, if at all possible, try to avoid supporting minor suits in these sequences, since it is unlikely that five of a minor is the only makable game contract Here partner will surely not raise, as his diamonds have to be of very poor quality. Instead, he may be able to show a maximum opener or even start cuebidding; remember your sequence is forcing and you are unlimited.

What about those decisions when partner shows an invitational hand with a long minor suit? Suppose, after your opening 1NT bid, partner responds 3♦ and you have the option to bid again on:

$$♠ A 6 5 \quad ♥ K J 8 \quad ♦ K J 6 \quad ♣ K 8 4 3$$

It is clear that partner has ♦AQxxxx and perhaps a queen or jack outside. That will give you six diamond tricks, but it is unlikely that you can organize three more before opponents break through in whatever suit they lead. A pass seems sensible.

Remember the importance of aces in notrump contracts? This hand is very different on the same sequence:

You	Partner
1NT	3♦
?	

♠ A J 6
♥ A 6 4 2
♦ A 8 6
♣ K 6 4

There are six diamond tricks and two aces and there is every chance that you'll pick up one more trick on the lead. This time 3NT is a good bet.

You	Partner
1NT	3♦
?	

♠ A K
♥ J 8 6
♦ A 7 6 2
♣ A J 8 6

Here you are open in hearts but partner could have a heart card to go with his two diamond honors without being too strong for the 3♦ bid. Bidding 3♠ now clarifies this situation. You are prepared to play 4♦ if necessary; admittedly this contract might fail, but it is worthwhile to try for 3NT, especially at IMP scoring.

You	Partner
1NT	3♦
?	

♠ J 6 4
♥ A K Q 3
♦ K 6 5
♣ A 8 6

This is a similar situation, but on this hand, of course, you bid 3♥. Partner will bid 3♠ with a card there (you might be looking for a club honor), 3NT with something in clubs, and 4♦ with nothing significant outside his long suit.

Points to remember

1. Don't rush into the final contract when there is no need to do so. Often a temporizing bid will allow partner to make a better decision about where to play.
2. Point count is not the only factor when considering partner's game invitation. Look at where your tricks are going to come from, and how quickly you can develop them. Remember the importance of aces.

Bidding over a 2NT opening

The problem when you open 2NT is that, even though everything starts one level higher, your bidding structure really needs to accomplish many of the same objectives that you have after a 1NT opening. Again, there are numerous ways of using transfers and Stayman variants, but I suggest not worrying about five-card majors in the big hand and adopting the following for simplicity:

3♣	Baron: partner is expected to bid his four-card suits up the line or to bid 3NT if his only four-card suit is clubs.
3♦	Transfer to hearts with possible slam interest (but see below).
3♥	Transfer to spades with possible slam interest.

It is common to play 3♣ as Stayman, of course, but Baron is a slightly more useful tool for slam exploration in terms of finding 4-4 minor fits. If you play Stayman, it is common over a 3♦ response to play 3♥ or 3♠ to show exactly four of the suit bid and five of the other major (the Smolen convention).

If you play major-suit transfers, you need to decide how to use 2NT-3♠, just like you did 1NT-2♠. Many of the same possibilities are there: a single-suit minor transfer, minor-suit Stayman, four-way transfers, and so on. I like to simplify things, and play that 3♠ shows a game-forcing hand with five spades and four hearts. If I transfer to hearts and then bid spades, it shows a 4-5 hand, while transferring to spades and bidding hearts shows 5-5 or better.

Any bid over partner's 2NT is forcing, of course, and you should decide in advance what you are going to bid on the next round after partner's anticipated reply. The method of scoring may well be relevant. However, here's a common problem situation. Partner opens 2NT and you hold:

♠ K 8 6   ♥ J   ♦ 8 5 4   ♣ A J 10 8 6 4

Before we discuss my recommended response, a new tip needs to be introduced. It is one of the most important, but even those who own pets ignore it with alarming regularity.

The tail should NOT wag the dog!

Even recognized 'good' players ignore this one. Picking up my usual lousy cards, I can almost rely on the fact that, when one opponent picks up a strong two-bid, his partner, at the slightest provocation, will launch into Blackwood, and on receiving the reply, take a decision on the final contract based on that one piece of information alone, while knowing little else about the big hand.

Dog-wagging is about as sensible as a penniless pauper walking down Millionaires' Row and knocking on doors to give the occupants helpful advice on their financial affairs; yet it goes on constantly. In this connection, the hand above illustrates a bee which has been buzzing in my bonnet for some time. The vast majority of players agree that raising 1NT or 2NT to 4NT is quantitative — very sensible, as no suit has been agreed. They therefore use the Gerber convention, 4♣, to ask for aces. You can see where I am heading. I would suggest that opposite a 15-17 1NT, Gerber is ludicrous, and opposite a 2NT opening (or, even worse, a 2♣ opening and a 2NT rebid), it is nothing short of lunatic. Yes, I know you can construct hands such as:

♠ 6   ♥ K Q J 6 4 2   ♦ K Q 8 5 4   ♣ 4

or the like where aces are your only interest but how often do they come up in any circumstances, never mind opposite a big notrump hand? Surely there's a better use for the 4♣ bid? Let's look at that hand again:

♠ K 8 6   ♥ J   ♦ 8 5 4   ♣ A J 10 8 6 4

Opposite a 2NT opening, anything up to 7♣ could be on - or there
may be no slam at all. Some players solve the problem by bidding
3♣ and then 4♣, but that sequence is far better used as a cuebid,
agreeing whatever suit partner bid over 3♣ and showing a club control. This hand is best shown by a direct, natural 4♣, game-forcing
obviously and showing slam interest. Opener can now cuebid and
should normally do so or, at any stage, can sign off in 4NT or 5♣.
Note that, in these minor-suit sequences, 4NT should always be
considered natural and passable particularly important at pairs.

   Now try bidding these hands, assuming partner opens 2NT; in
each case, think about how you expect the auction to continue.

a)   ♠ J 7 5   b) ♠ K Q 8 7 4   c) ♠ K 9 8 6 3
     ♥ Q 7   ♥ K 4   ♥ A Q
     ♦ K J 8 6 4 2   ♦ K 8 5   ♦ 8
     ♣ K 8   ♣ 9 7 5   ♣ J 9 6 4 2

a) If you follow my advice, you'll be able to bid a direct 4♦ and let
partner take charge. Many partnerships play 4♦ and 4♥ as Texas
major-suit transfers, allowing similar sequences to the ones after a
1NT opening. However, I strongly advise that 4♦ is better used
for slam-minded diamond hands. Remember that if partner now
bids 4NT, it is natural and for play.

b) Here, slam prospects depend on opener's overall strength and
his attitude to spades. Show your hand by transferring to spades with
3♥ and then bidding 4NT, again natural and invitational. Partner
now has a number of options: pass, sign off in 5♠, 6♠ or 6NT,
cuebid at the five-level or invite you to slam with 5NT. With nothing extra and poor intermediates, you would probably pass the invitation.

c) Here again you will bid 3♥ to transfer to spades, but what then?
Your clubs are poor but you have five of them and no reason to
suppress the suit. If your partner has ♠Ax or ♠Qx, you will need
ruffs to set up the spade suit without losing unnecessary tricks and
6♣ may be the only successful slam. If, after your 4♣ rebid, partner
rejects both your suits with a natural 4NT, accept his decision.

Points to remember
1.   Don't be tempted to 'take over' when partner has a very strong hand.
2.   I recommend abandoning Gerber and Texas over a 2NT opening bid,
         and instead using 4♣ and 4♦ as natural minor-suit slam tries.

3

In the slam zone

As was hinted in the last chapter, perhaps the most common errors in slam bidding involve players rushing into Blackwood or a similar gadget when cuebidding or making a descriptive bid like a splinter would have been more appropriate. We shall discuss Blackwood and some of its variants in detail at the end of this chapter but now we're going to begin by looking at some situations that arise after a one-level opening, where there has been one of the following:

1) A direct raise of opener's major, either natural or conventional.

2) A jump in a new suit, usually at the two-level, by responder, played as natural and game-forcing.

3) A new suit bid by responder followed by any of these rebids by opener: a jump in a new suit; a notrump rebid; a jump raise; a jump rebid of his own suit.

We'll also see how some of the previous tips apply here, and we'll come across some new ones as well. Assume that neither side is vulnerable and that we are sitting South at matchpoint scoring.

Raises and jump shifts

You open 1♥ and partner makes a non-forcing, invitational (constructive rather than preemptive) limit raise to 3♥. You have to find a rebid on:

♠ A K 8   ♥ A J 7 6 5   ♦ J 8 7 2   ♣ 4

Here 4♥ will be easy if partner can help with your diamond losers, but not if he has significant club wastage. Unfortunately, there's no way to find out if partner's cards are in the right place in this auction — all you can do is evaluate the quality of your own hand, and take a guess. In this case, you would look at your three quick tricks, hope that your club singleton is worth something, and bid 4♥. However, bridge is not generally a game where we want to guess if we don't have to. As a result, one method that is gaining some popularity is to use the 2NT response to a major to show a limit raise or better. This frees up bids below three of your major to be used as game tries; however, it sacrifices the useful slam-going sequences after a game-forcing 2NT, so it is probably not to be recommended.

You	Partner
1♥	3♥
?	

♠ 8 7 6 4
♥ A K Q 6 4
♦ Q 7 5
♣ Q

No game tries are available, so again it's guessing time. My view this time would be that it is unlikely that the two minor-suit queens are pulling their weight, or that partner can cover all the losers in spades and diamonds. Added to that, you probably have overkill in trumps, partner's likely ♥J being a wasted value. I would pass 3♥.

You	Partner
1♥	3♥
?	

♠ —
♥ A Q J 7 5
♦ K Q 8 6 4
♣ K Q 8

Still the same auction, but with this hand you want to make a move toward slam, and it costs nothing to bid 3♠ to show first-round control of spades on the way to game. Partner is expected to cuebid a minor-suit ace, if he has one, with 4♣ or 4♦. An additional possible agreement, which I like a lot, is to use 3NT by partner now (which should not now be a serious candidate for final contract) to show both minor aces; this saves a lot of bidding space.

You can see that it's easy to have a cooperative auction where both of you will be involved in the final decision on whether to bid a slam. Yet this is exactly the sort of hand on which many players cannot wait to fly into Blackwood. But, what happens if you do? If partner shows one ace, the slam will be worth bidding if his ace is in a minor suit but not if it is in spades. If partner shows two aces, a small slam will be worth bidding (probably, at worst, depending on catching the ♥K) but the grand slam will be there if he has both minor aces and the ♥K — only eleven points and well within the range of his bid. Again, Blackwood gives you little idea of what the right action is.

You	Partner
1♥	3♥
?	

♠ K Q 7
♥ A K J 7 4
♦ K 8 6 4 2
♣ —

You will certainly be playing in at least 4♥ and there are two possible approaches here. One is to make a natural bid in diamonds; the other is to cuebid spades or clubs. I favor bidding your suit here. If you bid 4♦, partner will realize that you cannot be making a slam try with no black-suit controls. You must therefore have bypassed them in favor of directing his attention to diamonds. Any diamond values (such as ♦QJx) in partner's hand will be priceless, while the club void can always be shown later if partner makes encouraging noises. If partner has good diamonds, it may not even matter if he does have the ♣A; on the other hand, if he doesn't have a diamond fit, slam is very unlikely.

Most players are taught to cuebid first-round controls in order to make a try for slam, showing second-round controls later on in the auction if necessary. However, this can be a serious space-waster, especially in a slam exploration that is starting at the four-level (after 1♠-3♠, for example). It is more efficient to cuebid both first- and second-round controls, using a Blackwood variant later on to check that you're not off two aces. Thus on this hand, instead of bidding 4♦, you could choose to cuebid 3♠, hoping that you don't hear a club cuebid from partner!

You	Partner
1♥	3♥
?	

♠ A 9 8
♥ K Q J 7 4 3
♦ —
♣ A Q J 5

Once more you have the choice of 4♣ or 3♠ and again, I prefer 4♣ though now it is less clear. As always, you need to try to anticipate where the auction is headed. The advantage of bidding 4♣ is that you find out right away if partner has diamond wastage. If he bids 4♦, you can choose between optimism (4♠) and pessimism (4♥). If he doesn't bid 4♦, you could be making a grand slam!

If, instead, you bid 3♠, partner bids 4♣, and you press on with 4♦, he is unlikely to bid on beyond game whatever he has. He doesn't know you're this good, and he probably doesn't have very good hearts.

You	**Partner**
1♥	3♥
?	

♠ A K 7
♥ J 8 6 5 3
♦ A Q 6
♣ A 8

Here, your prime concern is the quality of partner's trumps. The way to clarify this is to bid 5♥, specifically asking partner to look at his trumps. He should raise to slam with two honors or better or with one top honor and extra length — ♥ Axxxx for example.

Turning to the jump shift, you open 1♦ and partner responds 2♥ (game-forcing) What do you rebid now on:

♠ 10 8 7 6 ♥ K J ♦ K Q J 7 6 ♣ A 3

The general guide commonly taught is to bid exactly what you would have over a one-level response, except that it will obviously be at a level higher. This is advantageous in terms of ease of memory but shows an alarming lack of appreciation of the situation. In the old days, a jump-shift would be made on any kind of very strong hand — for example, a balanced twenty-count. The modern style is simply to make a normal response on this type of hand, using fourth-suit forcing or some such convention to set up a game force later on, rather than using up bidding space unnecessarily. The jump shift is generally reserved for a *one-suited* hand; furthermore that suit must be of excellent quality — my recommended test for this is 'Are you happy to have this suit as trumps facing a low doubleton?' The jump-shift suit may, however, be slightly weaker if partner intends to support the suit that you opened.

For this reason, as opener, unless you have a big two-suiter with the second suit very strong, you should not be looking for a fit in one of the unbid suits. In the above example, your final contract will be in one of the red suits and the last thing you want partner to do is devalue shortness in spades. It is therefore worse than useless to bid spades now. Instead, give partner as much useful information as possible by rebidding the excellent diamond suit with 3♦. Unless partner now raises diamonds, you will support hearts later — partner's suit should be at least six to the ace-queen.

Now try these examples on the same sequence:

	You	**Partner**
	1♦	2♥
	?	

a) ♠ 10 5 4 2   b) ♠ 10 8   c) ♠ A K 9 5
   ♥ A J   ♥ K Q 4 2   ♥ A 8 6
   ♦ Q J 6 4 2   ♦ K Q 8 5 3   ♦ K 9 7 5 4
   ♣ A Q   ♣ Q 7   ♣ A 3

a) With poorer diamonds than on our last example, bidding 3♦ is less clear and raising partner to 3♥ seems preferable. Let partner take it from there. (3♦ is certainly better than 2♠, though).

b) Here you will be supporting hearts and I recommend that you warn partner of your minimum strength and lack of aces by a direct jump to 4♥. This 'unnecessary' jump to game in a game-forcing situation, deliberately wasting bidding space, gives partner a very definite message — you have hearts, but you want to stop. ***Unnecessary rush is a signal to hush!*** If he persists, any cuebid you make now will show a *second-round* control.

c) Here you have every prospect of a slam and you will want to keep the bidding as low as possible to conserve space. You now have no reason to suppress your excellent spade holding and you should bid 2♠. When you support hearts later, partner will realize that you had a definite message to send him.

Even played in the modern style, jump shifts don't come up that often, and as a result, Bergen raises of major-suit openings have become popular. Using this method, after an opening bid of one of a major a raise to the three-level in that suit is preemptive and shows 0-6 points with at least four trumps. A jump shift to a minor also shows four-card trump support with a point-count as follows:

     3♣   7 to a poor 10 points.
     3♦   good 10-12 points.
(These bids say nothing about the minor suit named.)

This leaves the single raise to the two-level as showing a relatively weak hand. In systems that use a forcing 1NT response, there are sequences to show forward-going hands below the limit raise range, and also to show hands with limit raise values but only three-card trump support. 1♠-3♥ remains a natural game-forcing jump shift although some partnerships (notably those who play two-over-one as game-forcing) prefer to play it as a splinter.

After a Bergen raise, opener has an approximate idea of the combined point-count and can make a game try if there is room. The most difficult case arises after 1♥-3♦ when opener has to make an immediate decision between bidding 3♥ and going on to game. The easiest auction is 1♠-3♣, when opener has plenty of room to investigate. Where more than one intervening bid is available, it can be used either as a conventional or a natural game try. Such bids can, of course, also be used as advance cuebids on slam-going hands; the situation becomes clear if opener presses on to game or makes another cuebid after responder signs off at the three-level. A couple of examples will illustrate:

Opener	Partner
1♥	3♣
3♦	3♥
3♠	?

Here opener has, in the first place, asked for strength but, on hearing partner is minimum, has continued anyway. The diamond and spade bids are now revealed as cuebids. Responder is now invited to cuebid a minor-suit control, or to sign off again in 4♥.

Opener	Partner
1♥	3♦
3♥	3♠
4♦	?

Opener has cuebid controls in hearts and diamonds while denying a club control (having bypassed 4♣).

Try the following examples of Bergen-raise auctions assuming that you have this hand:

♠ A 8 6 4   ♥ J 5 3   ♦ A 6 4 2   ♣ 10 3

Choose your next bid in each of the following sequences:

a)	1♠	3♦	b)	1♠	3♦	c)	1♠	3♦	d)	1♠	3♦
	3♥	?		3♥	3♠		3♥	3♠		3♥	3♠
				4♣	?		4♦	?		4♥	?

a) You have shown a good 10-12 but are minimum in that range. Despite your two aces, you should simply sign off in 3♠.

b) The bidding now continues and partner has persisted with a cuebid of 4♣ so that he has now shown controls in hearts and clubs. You have no problem here; you can show your diamond control with 4♦, still below game.

c) Here partner has shown controls in both red suits while denying a club control. If your style is only to cuebid first-round controls as this stage, the diamond control is clearly a void and your ♦A is wasted. If your partnership cuebids first- or second-round controls, neither of you can handle clubs. In either case, you should sign off in 4♠.

d) Now partner has emphasized hearts while denying much in the minors and the position is less clear as you will have to go past game to show your useful ♦A. However, the ♠A is a valuable card that you don't have to have; partner should be able to underwrite the five-level given his bidding so far, and I would recommend pressing on with 5♦. Remember, partner was aware that he was encouraging you go past 4♠ when he bid 4♥; *he* is responsible.

Opener's rebids

Jump shifts by opener can create issues too. Again, many players would do well to remember the old Latin tag — *festina lente* (hasten slowly).

Partner	**You**
1♥	1♠
3♦	?

♠ A 9 7 3
♥ K J 6
♦ K 7 5
♣ 6 5 4

Here you have tremendous support for partner in both suits and every prospect of a slam; even the ♠A is likely to be useful as a control. For the moment, however, all that is needed is a quiet preference to 3♥, awaiting further developments. There is no need to rush; the bidding will not end here.

Partner	**You**
1♥	1♠
3♦	?

♠ J 7 5 2
♥ Q 7
♦ K 8 6
♣ 8 6 4 3

Here you will bid 3♥ again, giving false preference this time, but for a totally different reason. It may well be that 3NT is the only makable game and, if partner bids it now, you can pass. In the first example, if partner's next bid were 3NT, you would make an encouraging noise with 4♦ and partner would realize that you had slam ambitions.

Partner	**You**
1♥	1♠
3♦	?

♠ K 6 5 2
♥ 8
♦ A Q 3 2
♣ A 6 4 2

Here, you have a clear diamond raise but a cuebid of 4♣ saves space. You would never introduce clubs as a natural suit in this auction. Partner will assume that diamonds have been agreed unless you subsequently correct to hearts.

Where opener jumps to 2NT after a one-level response, this shows about 18-19 points:

Partner	**You**
1♥	1♠
2NT	?

♠ K J 7 5 3
♥ Q J 3
♦ 8 6 5
♣ 9 8

Here you just should sign off in 4♥ — you have no interest in any other contract.

Partner	**You**
1♥	1♠
2NT	?

♠ A 9 7 3
♥ J 4 3
♦ K 4
♣ A J 7 4

Partner is likely to have a 2-5-3-3 type hand and a slam could well be on. However, there is no need to rush. A simple 3♥, game forcing, is all that is needed. Partner may again bid 3NT with a poor suit and we may be well warned that a slam is not on. Otherwise he is invited to cuebid, bearing in mind that you are unlimited.

Partner	**You**
1♥	1♠
2NT	?

♠ K Q 9 7 4
♥ A 7
♦ K Q 8 5
♣ 9 7

It is likely that you are going bid a slam here but there is no need to rush, as any non-club denomination is possible. Simply bid 3♦ (a new suit at the three-level is obviously forcing in this situation), and await further developments.

Partner	You
1♥	1♠
2NT	?

♠ K J 6 3
♥ Q J 8
♦ A J 8
♣ Q 4 2

With partner having shown 18-19, you should make a quantitative raise to 4NT, planning to play there or in 6NT. With a flat hand, there is little or nothing to be gained by playing in hearts, while being in notrump could be critical at pairs.

Let's turn now to auctions where opener jump raises responder's suit. Note that, though very strong, this auction is not forcing so you can pass if you want to, although you will strive to bid game if you possibly can. Most of the hands that give you a problem will be those on which you have to figure out the best way to make your slam try.

Partner	You
1♣	1♥
3♥	3♠
4♦	?

♠ A K 3
♥ A K 7 4 3
♦ Q 4
♣ J 4 2

This is very likely to be a slam hand but Blackwood is out of order. Partner had the opportunity to cuebid clubs but failed to do so. If this denies a club control, you must sign off in 4♥. If partner could still have a second-round club control, you have two choices: cuebid 4♠, or jump to 5♥. This time the jump to five of your major asks specifically about second-round control of the suit neither of you has yet cuebid. We've seen how a bid of five of a major could show the other extreme — poor trumps and excellent side-suit controls. You can safely play the bid as two-way, though — it will normally be clear what is meant.

In fact, although we're getting a little ahead of ourselves, it can have a third meaning. If the opponents have bid, and neither you nor partner has cuebid their suit, a jump to five of your agreed major asks about second-round control of the opponents' suit. Again, it will always be pretty obvious what you mean.

Partner	You
1♥	1♠
3♠	?

♠ A K 7 5
♥ Q 3 2
♦ A K 4 2
♣ 9 8

With only third-round controls in clubs and hearts, Blackwood is out of order. A cuebid of 4♦ is all that is needed. Let partner take it from there.

Partner	You
1♥	1♠
3♠	?

♠ A K Q J 7 4
♥ 7
♦ K Q 8 5
♣ 9 7

This is getting closer to a legitimate Blackwood hand but again the useless doubleton in clubs makes it inadvisable. In contrast to the last hand, you have two good second-round controls and while 5♠ is not a bad idea, an alternative is to 'steal' a control with 4♦ and test partner's reaction. You can bid 5♠ later, pinpointing the club weakness.

Partner	You
1♥	1♠
3♠	?

♠ K Q J 6 3 2
♥ Q 8
♦ A J 8 6 4
♣ —

There are three possible approaches here. One is simply to bid your controls up the line as usual, starting with 4♣. Over 4♥, you will bid 5♣, showing second-round control in the suit and implying a diamond control. Partner will then have the chance to show a second-round control in either red suit, after which you will have to take a decision. Another possibility is to bid 4♦ now, and if partner bids 4♥, bid 6♣, clarifying the void. A third option is to bid 5♣ immediately, also clarifying the void. A case can be made for any of the three but the second is my preference.

What about situations where partner jump rebids a minor after you have responded in a major at the one-level? Now you have to consider game contracts in notrump, your major or partner's minor. Bear in mind that opener's rebid is non-forcing and you can pass it, or even if you bid on, stop in four of his minor. A slam will be under consideration only if the bidding progresses above four of partner's minor.

Partner	You
1♦	1♠
3♦	?

♠ K Q 7 3
♥ A 3
♦ K Q 4 3
♣ J 4 3

There is certainly potential for 6♦ here and you can agree diamonds and initiate cuebidding with an immediate 4♦, which is forcing. It saves space, however, to bid 3♥ now, intending to remove 3NT to 4♦ so that the 3♥ becomes an advance cuebid. Note that, by not bidding 2♥, partner has denied a four-card heart suit so he is unlikely to raise you to 4♥. Even if he does, a correction to 5♦ clarifies your intentions.

Partner	You
1♦	1♠
3♦	?

♠ A J 8 7 4
♥ 7
♦ K 8 5
♣ A Q 9 7

Again a diamond slam is likely and you can make an immediate cuebid of 4♣. This is customarily played as a cuebid in this sequence as opposed to a second suit.

Partner	You
1♦	1♠
3♦	?

♠ A K J 7 5
♥ —
♦ K Q 4 2
♣ 9 8 5 2

Here anything up to 7♦ could be on, although 5♦ could also be going down if partner has weak clubs. This hand is best shown by a void-showing splinter bid of 4♥. Remember 3♥ here is forcing, so the 'unnecessary' jump carries a clear message. Partner will be well placed to bid on from there.

Partner	You
1♦	1♠
3♦	?

♠ A K Q 6 3
♥ Q 5 3
♦ —
♣ A Q 5 4 2

So what now? It should be appreciated that as good as your hand is, a slam is unlikely. Give partner about sixteen points and there are thirty-three in total — but a complete misfit. One approach is to accept your fate gracefully and sign off in 3NT. Probably better, however, is to try 3♠, played as forcing nowadays. This still leaves the option of 3NT open but partner could still have three spades; if he raises you can look for the only likely slam in 6♠. Ruffs are likely to be needed to set the long diamonds up.

Blackwood

Yes, finally I'm going to talk about it — and even advise you to use it! Remember that the Blackwood convention is primarily a safety device; its primary use is to keep you out of bad slams, not to propel you into good ones. It is your final check to ensure that you're not missing two aces once you have already determined through other bidding that slam prospects are good, and that you have at least second-round control of all suits. Do not use Blackwood or any of its variants unless you are ready to deal with any answer to 4NT and are sure you will know what final contract to bid. Once you use Blackwood, partner should accept your decision as to the final contract. Thus the convention should normally be used by the stronger hand who has more information than his weaker counterpart.

As a general rule, 4NT is only Blackwood when it is clear that a suit has been agreed. Thus a suit will have been bid and supported or the inquirer will suddenly jump to 4NT, clarifying that the last suit his partner bid is the suit agreed. Otherwise 4NT is natural — this is particularly important with minor-suit hands at pairs.

The time to use it arises when you have plenty of second-round controls, kings and singletons. It is out of order with voids (when aces may be valueless), or with doubletons and queen-high holdings when, if partner fails to produce the ace, the king may be missing as well and you will have two top losers.

There are many popular variants of Blackwood and it's worth looking at some of them.

Original — ace-asking in response to 4NT

5♣	0 or 4 aces
5♦	1 ace
5♥	2 aces
5♠	3 aces

After that, 5NT can be used in a similar manner for kings although most play 6NT to show all four, the partnership now surely committed to the seven-level.

When responding to any version of Blackwood, useful voids may be shown by bidding the same suit as you would have bid at the five-level but at the six-level instead. Responder should be sure that the void will be useful — be reluctant to show a void in partner's bid suit, as it may well be more of a hindrance than a help.

Economy ace-asking

5♣	0 or 3 aces
5♦	1 or 4 aces
5♥	2 aces of the same rank
5♠	2 aces: club/heart or diamond/spade
5NT	2 aces: same color

This is an improvement on the original Roman Blackwood responses where 5♥ showed two aces of the same color or rank and 5♠ showed two non-matching aces. However, the disadvantage here lies in the possible loss of the 5NT bid for kings.

Note there is scope for ambiguity when a Blackwood response has more than one meaning, but it is usually clear whether responder has the lower or higher number of aces from the bidding to date. It is, however, fitting to recall a team of world champions who, on one occasion, bid a grand slam with all four aces missing. They had a good laugh about it, wrote down the penalty and got on with the next hand!

Roman Key Card Blackwood

Here, the king of trumps is considered the fifth 'ace':

5♣	0 or 3 'aces'
5♦	1 or 4 'aces'
5♥	2 or 5 'aces' without the queen of trumps
5♠	2 or 5 'aces' with the queen of trumps

This showing of the queen of trumps is very helpful where the partnership has only eight trumps between them, typically after a Stayman sequence. After a 5♣ or 5♦ response, there are extended sequences to inquire about the trump queen. Some prefer to define the 5♥ and 5♠ bids as distinguishing between no extra values or extra values (of which the trump queen would be a typical example).

Exclusion Blackwood

This variant emphasizes the need to show useful aces, commonly after one of the partnership has shown a splinter (specifically a void) and bid 4NT. Responder is expected to exclude the ace of that short suit from his calculations. Unusual jumps to the five-level can be used as Exclusion Blackwood also, the suit bid being the excluded suit.

Romex

This is another way of responding that includes provision for voids:

5♣	0 or 3 aces
5♦	1 or 4 aces
5♥	2 aces
5♠	1 ace and a spade void

5NT   2 aces and any useful void
6 suit   1 ace and a void in the suit bid
6 trumps 1 ace and a void in a suit higher-ranking than the
               trump suit

There are a number of other variants of Blackwood on the scene but, as I have already indicated, I am not very keen on most of them. Roman Key Card is certainly the most popular today and it's probably the best.

Points to remember

1. When making a slam try, think ahead to where the auction is going. Pick the bid that will prompt to partner to give you the information you most want.

2. Consider agreeing to cuebid both first- and second-round controls, to make efficient use of space in cuebidding auctions. You can check on aces later before finally bidding your slam.

3. Consider using an advance cuebid to conserve space, instead of simply raising partner in a forcing auction.

4. ***Don't drift after a jump shift!*** If partner forces to game by jumping in a new suit, assume that one of the two bid suits will be trumps or that game will be played in 3NT. Do not bid a new suit attempting to find a fit elsewhere but, by all means, show it in advance of supporting partner if the information will be useful in assessing slam prospects.

5. A jump to the five-level in the agreed major usually asks for second-round control of the unbid suit (or the opponents' suit if they have bid). If it obviously cannot be that, it asks about trump quality

6. Avoid Blackwood except as a final check on the number of aces partner holds, when that is the *only* thing you need to be sure of to bid a slam. Do not bid Blackwood with a void, or when you are not yet certain that you have at least second-round control of all suits.

4

To the moon, Alice!

This will be the last chapter before we allow the opponents to enter the fray. I mentioned at the beginning of this book that preemptive bidding is rampant nowadays, and there is much discussion in bridge literature regarding how to bid over it. Relatively little, however, has been written on how the preemptor's partner bids over it, especially when he has a good hand. We shall concentrate on situations where the preemptive bid has been made in first or second position, i.e. where partner is unlimited. In third position, anything seems to go nowadays and these auctions will not be discussed at this stage; the fourth hand will almost invariably compete and we are still talking about bidding against silent opposition.

Opening a preempt

Firstly, we need to discuss when you should preempt, and on what kind of hand. Needless to say, opinions vary widely on these topics. Let's start by looking at opening bids at the three-level. Obviously, the vulnerability of each side is highly relevant as we are at least theoretically offering the opponents a chance for a penalty. We need to consider how good the suit has to be and what limit we put on side-suit holdings, i.e. what partner can assume about our defensive prospects. My recommended rules are on the conservative side.

In contrast to many modern players, I do not preempt at the three-level with a six-card suit — I open a weak two-bid. There are two issues for me. If you open at the three-level on a six-bagger and it is a good suit, AQxxxx say, it may be worth two defensive tricks; not expecting this, partner may sacrifice at the wrong moment. If it is a poor suit and they double you, the penalty could be huge; worse still, partner may lead from something like Kx to find you with Jxxxxx or lead from Ax opposite Qxxxxx and present an unmakable game or slam to the opponents. It happens often. So, although many players consider a six-card suit (and some even five!) to be enough at favorable vulnerability, I'm going to assume here that a three-level preempt promises a seven-card suit to at least one of the top three honors. The overall strength required depends on vulnerability; we shall assume approximate adherence to the rule of 500 — the traditional anticipation of a double and then a three-trick set when not vulnerable or a two-trick set vulnerable.

My second rule is that I prefer not to have more than one defensive trick outside my preempt suit. There are partnerships who insist merely on no ace outside — too inflexible for me. It is a cardinal error to preempt with 'soft' defensive values outside your own suit — those queens and jacks will be of little use to you if you get doubled, but may make all the difference in the world to whether or not they can make anything.

For me, however, preempting at game level is a totally different ball-game and I tend to do it on stronger hands than most. Look at:

♠ 7 ♥ A K Q 8 7 6 4 ♦ K J 5 ♣ 8 6

Thirteen points and possibly three or more defensive tricks, but nothing would make me open this at the one-level. Opponents could easily be cold for a slam in either black suit and I am going to make sure that they start discussing it at 4♠ at the cheapest. I have collected countless +590's and +790's through being doubled in these contracts, not to mention the occasional overtrick. This particularly applies in the modern scene where doubles of game preempts tend to be played to show 'general values' rather than being specifically for takeout; often, the doubler's partner passes for lack of somewhere to go. It has been said that 'A preempt that is known to be weak is a blunt weapon', but I find few players actually practice this — their preempts are either weak or extraordinarily weak!

Look at this rare example (which incidentally was hand- rather than computer-dealt). What do you open with neither side vulnerable at matchpoints on this:

♠ —   ♥ —   ◆ A K Q J 10 9 6 5 4   ♣ A 8 6 4

No system has a bid for this hand, and depending on the rest of the layout, almost anything could be right.   I have little doubt, however, that 6◆ is best with 5◆ a poor second.   I would prefer starting with 7◆ (let them guess whether I can make it!) to opening at a lower level.   The overriding consideration is your lack of defensive prospects.   Of course, on a dream day, partner will turn up with a diamond void and the opposing cards in the suit will split 2-2, giving you a likely three defensive tricks.   In your worst nightmare, the opponents will produce voids in both minors, leaving you totally defenseless.   To be realistic, you likely have one defensive trick or two if you are very lucky, and therefore giving the opponents as little room as possible is crucial.   The full deal actually was:

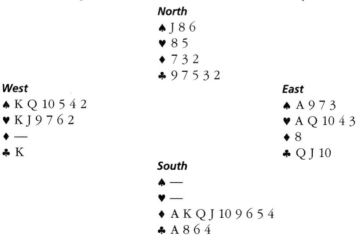

North
♠ J 8 6
♥ 8 5
◆ 7 3 2
♣ 9 7 5 3 2

West
♠ K Q 10 5 4 2
♥ K J 9 7 6 2
◆ —
♣ K

East
♠ A 9 7 3
♥ A Q 10 4 3
◆ 8
♣ Q J 10

South
♠ —
♥ —
◆ A K Q J 10 9 6 5 4
♣ A 8 6 4

I held the West hand and South opened a strong 2◆, allowing my partner and me the bidding room to get together and reach slam in a major.   The par contract is 7◆ doubled going down two for 300.   But think about West's problem over an opening bid of 6◆! Either bidding or not bidding could be very expensive.   The general tip on highly distributional hands is that, at teams, it usually pays to insist on playing the hand on the basis that it is best to aim for the *little* mistake — conceding a small minus instead of gaining a small plus, as opposed to conceding a game or slam instead of gaining one. At matchpoints, it is less clear, since any minus can be a disaster if the rest of the field have plus scores. Even if West does decide to bid over 6♦, what bid does he make? Bidding six of a major risks making the wrong choice, and how many pairs have a clear understanding on what double means here? Even if double is played as takeout, partner is likely to bid clubs. A cuebid of 7♦ will certainly say 'pick a major', but missing three aces West can guess that the seven-level is going to be too high.

Let's look at some more examples — for a change, we'll assume both sides are vulnerable, and that the scoring is IMPs. Each time, you are the dealer:

♠ Q J 10 8 7 5 3 ♥ — ♦ 9 ♣ A K J 7 4

It is anybody's guess how much defense you have here but, from long experience, I find that, unless the seven-card suit is very poor, it pays to treat these long major, shorter minor hands as one-suited; open 4♠ and let opponents guess. Yes, it will mean you miss the occasional slam (although only when partner feels he cannot underwrite the five-level) but the damage to the opponents will easily compensate. If you do open 1♠, what are going to bid over two of a red suit from partner, or even 1NT for that matter? It is most unlikely that you will want to play this hand in clubs and anyway, it is unclear how high you should bid the suit. To do the hand justice, you will have to give partner the impression of a much higher point-count than your actual eleven and, if he has a big hand with a misfit, you are almost certain to get too high.

♠ J 8 7 6 5 4 3 ♥ A K ♦ Q J 6 ♣ J

Here you have plenty of defense and a very poor suit and no reason to preempt. Just open 1♠ and keep rebidding the suit.

♠ 8 ♥ K Q J 8 6 4 ♦ Q J 8 6 4 3 ♣ —

With a moderate two-suiter, I prefer passing and waiting for opponents to bid the blacks after which you can come in with an unusual notrump to clarify the position. If partner bids a black suit, you will be glad you did not open; the same applies if the opponents bid a red suit which would devalue your hand considerably. A hand like this has enough playing strength to enter the auction at a high level, even at this vulnerability, and I recommend waiting to see how the land lies.

♠ Q 8 7 6 5 3 2   ♥ A 9   ♦ K 8   ♣ 9 6

Many people would open this at the one-level or the three-level, justifying their actions on losing trick count or some similar assessment. Again, I prefer to pass. There is plenty of defense and you can always come in later without raising the level of bidding. Partner should realize that you have this type of hand. One possibility is to open 2♠, but I prefer to reserve this for six-card suits only.

Bidding over partner's preempt

Everyone is vulnerable, and partner deals and opens 3♣. If you have a hand with some interest in moving forward, there are a number of approaches you can use; however, many partnerships have discussed little except that a new suit bid would be forcing. The following is a relatively simple but quite powerful structure that you might want to try:

1) On hands with a club fit, where you are frightened that opponents are cold for game or slam, you can extend the preempt by simply raising the clubs.

2) Where you have a good major suit of your own, and you have enough strength to play in 4♣ if necessary, you can bid your suit (natural and forcing) and now partner should either:

    i) Raise.

    ii) Cuebid a singleton or void in support of your suit.

    iii) At the three-level (if space permits), bid a side-suit feature for notrump; typically, after 3♣-3♥, a bid of 3♠ shows a spade stopper, and 3NT shows a diamond stopper; after 3♣-3♠, a bid of 3NT shows a red-suit stopper (which sadly cannot be specified). Note that there does not need to be any ambiguity at the three-level between a cuebid and a notrump stopper; if you make a cuebid and partner bids 3NT, thinking you were showing a stopper, you will correct to four of his major, clarifying the position.

    iv) Merely rebid his clubs if he has nothing further to say.

3) Where you are looking for 3NT — confident that you can bring

the club suit in and that it is a question of side-suit stoppers, you can use 3♦ as a forcing relay. Partner is now expected to reply as follows (working on the assumption that he has, at most, one side-suit stopped):

3♥	heart stopper
3♠	spade stopper
3NT	diamond stopper
4♣	no outside stopper

Does this all make sense? Some practice examples will help. Try these (you are South):

West	North	East	South
	3♣	pass	?

a) ♠ A K Q 6   b) ♠ 7 5 2   c) ♠ A Q J 6   d) ♠ 6 3 2
   ♥ 7 4   ♥ Q J 2   ♥ K Q 7 4   ♥ Q 8 7
   ♦ Q J 4 2   ♦ A K 4 2   ♦ 8 5   ♦ 9 6 4
   ♣ A J 4   ♣ A 9 8   ♣ K 9 7   ♣ K 8 6 5

In (a), (b), (c) you are expecting to bring in the club suit and require a stopper in the weak suit. On all three of these, you relay with 3♦, intending to play 3NT, if partner produces the stopper, or 4♣ if he doesn't. On hand (d) opponents could be cold for anything up to a grand slam. Your side is likely to make six or, more probably, seven tricks in clubs. I would bid 5♣ here at equal vulnerability, 4♣ at unfavorable, and 6♣ at favorable.

When partner opens 3♦, there is less space available below 3NT. My recommended, slightly modified, approach is as follows, the first priority of the partnership being the 3NT goal but four of a major or five of the minor need not be ruled out. Therefore, to preserve all your options, bid as follows:

3♥ — a heart suit or stopper; partner rebids as follows:

3♠	spade stopper
3NT	club stopper
4♣	no black-suit stopper but heart support; you will sign off in 4♦, 4♥ or 5♦ according to your hand.
4♦	no black-suit stopper and no heart support.

3♠ — a spade suit or stopper; partner rebids as follows:

    3NT   heart stopper (there is no room to show the club

stopper but against 3NT a major-suit lead is more likely, so the heart stopper takes priority)

4♣   no heart stopper but spade support; you will sign off in 4♦, 4♠ or 5♦ according to your hand.

4♦   no black-suit stopper and no heart support.

This is far from perfect in that, with three-card support for the major *and* a stopper, the opener has to make a choice, ignorant of responder's meaning. I recommend that the first priority should be showing the stopper — there may be another chance to show support later. Also, we are working on the assumption that the opener has no more than one side-suit stopped. There are rare occasions when he will have two, e.g. on a hand like this:

♠ —   ♥ Q 7 5   ♦ K Q 7 6 5 4 2   ♣ Q 8 4

If you have, in fact, preempted on this hand, I recommend that priority be given to showing the major-suit stopper as that suit is more likely to be led. With both major suits stopped, you were probably wrong to preempt in the first place.

Despite these potential problems, the method has worked very well for my students and I know of nothing significantly better that isn't a great deal more complex. So, try these examples where you are responding to partner's 3♦ preempt; again, think about whether your answer would change depending on vulnerability.

a)   ♠ A K Q   b) ♠ 7 5   c) ♠ A Q J 4
     ♥ 7 4   ♥ A Q J 2   ♥ K Q 7 4
     ♦ Q 4 2   ♦ K 4 2   ♦ —
     ♣ A Q J 4 2   ♣ A Q 9 8   ♣ A Q 9 7 5

a) Bid 3♠, expecting to play 3NT or 5♦ according to the answer. If partner is liable to preempt very light at favorable vulnerability, you might settle for 4♦ but I suggest that you should go for game in all circumstances.

b) Similar — this time you bid 3♥.

c) A disturbing number of players would bid 3NT without a second thought on the basis of 'having the other suits stopped, partner!' But how are you going to make it when you may have to make all nine tricks in your own hand? At unfavorable vulnerability there is a case for trying 5♦, which may make; however, partner failed to open a Gambling 3NT (discussed later), which is usually appropriate on a solid minor suit, so trump losers are almost certain. I recommend passing whatever the vulnerability. When this hand came up in a European tournament, both sides were vulnerable; among scores of tables, I was the only player who passed 3♦. Partner just scraped home for the only plus score in our direction.

When the preempt is in a major suit, the prime goal is four of that major, but 3NT is not ruled out. If responder bids a new suit at the four-level (natural or an advance cuebid, and certainly forcing), 3NT is now ruled out and the preemptor, with the partnership already committed to at least the major-suit game, is expected to cuebid a control or shortness with a view to a slam. Again, note the emphasis on the goal.

In situations where responder is weak and has a fit in the preemptive suit, he should raise as high as possible with a view to conceding a small enough penalty to show a profit against the opponents' most likely contract (probably at least game but perhaps as much as a grand slam). Now vulnerability is invariably critical.

Partner opens 3♥; what do you reply on:

a) ♠ A K Q 6 b) ♠ K 5 2   c) ♠ A K J 10 4 d) ♠ 6 3 2
   ♥ —   ♥ A J 2   ♥ K Q 7   ♥ Q 8 7 5
   ♦ A Q J 4 2   ♦ K 4 2   ♦ 10 8 5 3 2   ♦ 9 6 4
   ♣ A Q 9 4   ♣ A 9 8 7   ♣ —   ♣ A K 8

Would the vulnerability make any difference?

Partner opens 3♠; what do you reply on:

e) ♠ 6   f) ♠ K 5 2   g) ♠ A J 4   h) ♠ 9 6 3 2
   ♥ A J 7 4   ♥ A Q J 2   ♥ A K Q J 10 8   ♥ 9 8 7 5
   ♦ Q J 4 2   ♦ A K J 2   ♦ 8 5   ♦ 9 4
   ♣ A J 4 2   ♣ A 8   ♣ A 7   ♣ 10 8 6 5

Again, would the vulnerability make any difference?

a) By now you should have been cured of bidding 3NT but, even if two or three trump tricks have to be lost, 4♥ should be an excellent contract. At unfavorable vulnerability, since partner's hearts may well be good enough to play for one loser opposite a void, a case can be made for looking for a slam. The way to do that would be to bid a new suit, 3♠ say, and then to bid 5♥. Note that an immediate 5♥ after a preempt is merely extending the barrage, not inquiring about trump quality; partner should not bid again.

b) Now the hearts are coming in without a problem; this is the time to bid 3NT since there is little to be gained by playing in a trump suit — if you can rely on the quality of partner's suit for his preempt. A spade or diamond lead will almost certainly give you the contract at once. On a club or heart lead, at worst, you will need a little luck. But now look at 4♥ — you will have eight tricks on top but you may well need both the ♠A and the ♦A well placed. Worse still, your hand will be the dummy and the contract could go down right away on the wrong lead, even if one of those aces is well placed!

Notice that I am recommending supporting the suit on a void and advising against it with tremendous trumps, illustrating perfectly the importance of understanding the ideas behind the game rather than learning to apply 'rules' rigidly.

c) Here anything from 4♥ to 7♥ could be lay-down. Certainly a case could be made for shutting your eyes and bidding 6♥ out of hand, hoping for a favorable lead and/or the right diamond holding in partner's hand. Doubtless, this would be the approach of the bashers. However, let's watch the scientists in action. Over a natural forcing 3♠, partner is expected to bid 3NT with a stopper in either minor or 4♣ or 4♦ to show a minor-suit singleton or void. Without either, he signs off in 4♥. If partner bids 4♦, you can now try 5♣ to see if he bids 5♦ to confirm a void. Now 7♥ will, at worst, be on the spade finesse if partner produces three small in that suit.

d) One approach here would be to push up as high as you dare in hearts according to vulnerability. The alternative is to bid 4♣ to ensure the correct lead in case the hand on your left becomes declarer. This second approach has the disadvantage of giving the opponents more room and arguably warning them of impending trouble. At all vulnerabilities, I recommend bidding 4♥ here; you intend to allow 5♠ to play but you will bid 5♣ over their 4♠ to ensure the club lead against 5♠. Note again the emphasis on the goal, whether the hand is going to be played by you or your opponents!

e) This is another example where many players would go flying into 3NT without a second thought. To be fair, that contract will make if partner has seven solid spades and that is a possibility here if you are vulnerable. 4♠, however, is a far better chance. Now it is a certainty that a large number of spade tricks will be made and your intermediate honors in the other suits may produce an extra trick. If you're not vulnerable, I recommend passing; vulnerable, it is probably wise to pass at pairs but bid 4♠ at teams.

f) Not vulnerable, partner has promised six tricks and, at the worst, a small slam will need just a bit of luck. The same applies to a grand slam if partner is vulnerable. One approach is simply to bid it and leave it at that. However, in either case, it costs nothing to look around. Even not vulnerable, the grand slam could be on. Start with 4♣ and then bid 5♦ over the likely sign-off in 4♠. Partner can now show you second-round control in hearts or clubs if he has it and then you can make a decision.

g) This is another trap for the Blackwood addicts. Obviously, if partner shows an ace, you can bid the grand slam with confidence. But if he does not, you are little the wiser. Again, start cuebidding with 4♣. Assuming partner signs off in 4♠, bid 5♣ showing second-round control in clubs. I know you don't have it, but that's not serious. The important thing is to ensure that partner shows the second-round diamond control if he has it. Notice that it's okay to deceive partner as long as you are in control.

h) Here opponents may be cold for anything up to a grand slam and you must raise the level of the bidding according to vulnerability. I would bid 4♠ at unfavorable vulnerability, 5♠ at equal, and 6♠ at favorable.

The preemptor's rebid

Although some experts consider this too inflexible, it is a generally accepted principle that, once you have preempted, you should not bid again unless partner forces you to do so. In that case, he is responsible for any reply you make. The rationale behind this is straightforward. With your preemptive bid, you have more or less shown what you have and your partner should be taking the decision on the final contract, being in possession of far more information. Thus the following rules are normally applicable:

1) Any raise of your suit is merely there to extend the preempt and should be considered a sign-off. Partner should have travanced action against competition and you must respect his decision, right or wrong.

2) Any bid at the game level in any suit should be considered a sign-off. You should only bid in exceptional circumstances, typically with a fit in partner's suit and a void outside, when it is most likely

that you can underwrite the overtrick. On this kind of hand, you might want to cuebid the void. Note that this cannot be misunderstood as a second suit. Preemptive bids, particularly preempts below game, should show, in principle, *one-suited* hands.

Try the following examples where you have preempted as South, having dealt at game all at teams' scoring. In each case, you are using the bidding structure described in this chapter.

You open 3♣ and partner responds 3♦. What is your rebid on:

a) ♠ K 8 6	b) ♠ 5 2	c) ♠ 10 3	d) ♠ 6 3 2
♥ 8	♥ K 2	♥ J	♥ 5
♦ 4 2	♦ 4 2	♦ Q 10 8	♦ 94
♣ A J 10 9 7 5 3	♣ A 10 9 8 7 6 3	♣ K Q 8 6 4 3 2	♣ A K 10 8 6 4 2

Here the 3♦ relay asked you for notrump stoppers and you should show them as follows:

a) 3♠ to show the spade stopper;
b) 3♥ — heart stopper;
c) 3NT —diamond stopper;
d) 4♣ — to disappoint!

You open 3♣ and partner responds 3♥. What is your rebid on:

a) ♠ K 8 6	b) ♠ 5	c) ♠ 10 3
♥ 8	♥ K 8 2	♥ J
♦ 4 2	♦ 4 2	♦ Q 10 8
♣ A J 10 9 7 5 3	♣ A 10 9 8 7 6 3	♣ K Q 8 6 4 3 2

Partner's 3♥ is natural, showing at least a five-card suit, and you should give more information:

a) Bid 3♠ to show the spade stopper and no heart support — 3NT can still be on and, even if it is not, your bid may help partner decide whether to play in 4♣ or 5♣.
b) Here you are happy to raise to 4♥.
c) Bid 3NT — shows a diamond stopper and denies heart support.

You open 3♦ and partner responds 3♥. What is your rebid?

a) ♠ K 8 6	b) ♠ 5	c) ♠ 10 3	d) ♠ 7 6
♥ 8	♥ K 8 2	♥ 9	♥ J 8
♦ A J 10 7 5 3 2	♦ A J 8 7 5 4 3	♦ A Q 10 8 6 5 3	♦ A J 9 7 6 4 2
♣ 7 4	♣ 10 6	♣ K 3 2	♣ 6 2

Partner has shown either a heart suit or a feature for notrump:

    a) Bid 3♠ to show the spade stopper.

    b) Bid 4♣ to show no black-suit stopper but heart support. Partner will bid either 4♦ or 4♥, according to whether he had a real heart suit.

    c) Bid 3NT to show the club stopper.

    d) 4♦ to show no help anywhere.

You open 3♦ and partner responds 3♠. What is your rebid on each of these two hands:

	a)		b)
♠	Q 6 3	♠	K 5 2
♥	—	♥	8 7 6
♦	A K 8 7 6 4 2	♦	K Q J 8 7 4 2
♣	8 7 5	♣	—

Partner has shown a spade suit or a feature for notrump.

a) Here you are sensational and you can bid 4♥ — you are prepared to play in game in spades or diamonds. There are partnerships who play this type of bid to show either a singleton or void and certainly if you do, you will get to use the bid more often. I prefer to restrict this kind of bid to a void, winning on accuracy as, with the other method, partner does not know how to value an ace. With a singleton, you can always get active later if it becomes obvious that partner is worried about that suit.

b) Here again you are sensational but it would take a 5♣ bid to show the void as 4♣ is used to show spade support. The five-level may be too high and a straightforward 4♣ is recommended, prepared to cuebid clubs later if partner makes any encouraging noises.

We could go on for hours but this should be enough to illustrate my approach.

Points to remember

1. The preempt that is known to be weak is a blunt weapon. When you have little defense, don't be afraid to preempt with quite strong hands, especially at the game level.

2. Be conservative as to suit quality and length, whatever the vulnerability; that way partner will know how to value his own hand, either constructively, or when considering a sacrifice.

3. Discuss your bidding structure over preempts with your partner. One-third of the time when you preempt as dealer, partner will have a good

hand. You can use the structure described here, or something else that
you prefer.

4. Don't bid 3NT over partner's preempt just because you have good hand
   and no fit: think about where your tricks are coming from, and decide
   on the most likely making contract. It is often right to bid 3NT with a
   good fit for partner, but to raise his suit with fairly weak support!

5. Most important, note that the opener does not rebid his preemptive
   suit unless he has been forced *and* has no alternative. I lose count of the
   number of people who preempt and then repeat their suit, sometimes
   twice more, 'because I had seven of them, partner!' Rest assured, partner was listening the first time!

6. ***More than once and you're a dunce!*** Therefore, once you have preempted, do not repeat your suit except as a last resource; prefer to give
   partner further information, (specifically stoppers for notrump or shortness for slams), rather than tell him what he knows already!

7. A little mistake is better than a big one. Especially in team games, it is
   often right to take insurance in a competitive auction at a high level.
   You're better to bid one more and go down one than risk their making
   a game or slam if you think both sides may be able to make something.
   And they may bid again, too!

Gambling 3NT

Finally, we shall consider a special type of preempt — Gambling
3NT, a popular and useful convention which certainly comes up
more often than do balanced 25-27 point hands (the traditional
meaning of a 3NT opening). The Gambling 3NT opening shows a
solid minor suit (AKQxxxx should be considered minimum) and
not more than about a queen outside. The recommended responses
are as follows:

Pass	to play
4♣	to play or to be corrected to 4♦ if appropriate
4♦	indicates a willingness to play in five of the minor and asks opener to cuebid a singleton or void in a side suit. Opener now rebids as follows:

4♥	singleton or void heart
4♠	singleton or void spade
4NT	no singleton or void
5♣	singleton or void diamond
5♦	singleton or void club

4♥   to play
4♠   to play
5♣   pass or correct

This leaves the 4NT raise unassigned. I like to play this as showing a void in the minor and a colossal hand outside, typically something like this:

♠ A K Q 3   ♥ A K 6 2   ♦ —   ♣ A J 8 6 3

Now the quality of the opener's minor is crucial, and he rebids as follows:

5♣ or 5♦	having only AKQxxxx in that suit
6♣ or 6♦	having AKQJxxx or AKQxxxxx or better in the suit, i.e. no loser expected even opposite a void
5♦,5♥ or 5♠	a solid suit and the queen in the suit bid — this may be important as an entry to the long minor in 6NT or 7NT

This may sound complicated, but it isn't really, as the following examples will show. On each of the following set of hands, you are dealer with neither side vulnerable at pairs, and open 3NT. What are your rebids on these hands on each of the auctions that follow:

a) ♠ 8 6   b) ♠ 5 3   c) ♠ Q 3   d) ♠ 6
   ♥ 8 7   ♥ 8 2   ♥ 9   ♥ Q 8
   ♦ AKQ6532   ♦ AKQJ875   ♦ AKQ9653   ♦ AKQJ642
   ♣ 7 4   ♣ 10 6   ♣ 8 3 2   ♣ 6 3 2

e) ♠ 8 6   f) ♠ 10 3   g) ♠ Q 3 2   h) ♠ 6 5
   ♥ 8 7 4   ♥ 8 2   ♥ —   ♥ 9 8
   ♦ AKQ6532   ♦ AKQJ875   ♦ AKQJ653   ♦ AKQJ642
   ♣ 7   ♣ 10 6   ♣ 8 3 2   ♣ Q 3

Auction 1.   **You**   **Partner**
                   3NT   4♣
                   ?

Here partner has stated that he wishes to play at the four-level in your long minor. You simply correct to 4♦ on all eight hands.

Auction 2.   **You**   **Partner**
                   3NT   4♦
                   ?

Here he has asked for a singleton or void in any side suit. You answer with 4NT (none) on (a), (b), (f) and(h); 4♥ (heart shortage)
on (c) and g); 4♠ (spade shortage) on (d) and 5♦ (club shortage) on
(e).

Auction 3.	**You**	**Partner**
	3NT	4♥
	?	

Here he has expressed the wish to play 4♥. You have no reason to
remove the sign-off on any of these hands.

Auction 4.	**You**	**Partner**
	3NT	4♠
	?	

The same applies in 4♠ but on hand (g), I suggest that you cuebid
the heart void with 5♥ as you can surely underwrite 5♠; for all partner knew, you could have had a spade void and three small hearts.

Auction 5.	**You**	**Partner**
	3NT	4NT
	?	

Now partner is inquiring about your diamond strength. You should
show the minimum suit with 5♦ on hands (a), (c) and (e). You
show the good suit with no queen outside with 6♦ on hands (b) and
(f) and the good suit with an outside queen with 5♥ on (d), 5♠ on
(g) and 5♣ on (h).

Auction 6.	**You**	**Partner**
	3NT	5♣
	?	

This time partner has expressed the wish to play in game in your
minor. You correct to 5♦ on all eight hands.

Points to remember

1. Gambling 3NT is just like any other preempt — you need specific un-
    derstandings on suit quality and defensive values outside the suit be-
    fore you agree to play it.
2. Adopt a sensible constructive bidding structure over it, either the one sug-
    gested here or some other that you prefer.

Competitive Auctions

5

So who counts points, anyway?

From here on, we shall generously allow the opponents to take part in the bidding. As you have seen, plenty of mistakes are made in uncontested auctions. But the points thrown away in that area are a mere hors-d'oeuvre compared with the untold millions thrown to the winds in competitive auctions, as you will soon see. There is an instinct that leads many, particularly male players who overrate their own capabilities, to insist on declaring when they ought to be defending; equally culpable are those, admittedly a minority, who sway in the opposite direction. You have already learned to help partner in valuing his hand where possible. Hand evaluation is even more important when both sides are bidding and it is well worthwhile spending a chapter discussing it.

I lose count of the number of occasions that students need to be admonished for bidding too much on seventeen points or more when their hand has minimal trick-taking potential. **Seventeen or more points is not necessarily a good hand.** While writing this chapter, I came across the following example in a teams' event.

As South, with North-South vulnerable, you deal yourself:

♠ 8 7 ♥ A K J ♦ A J 7 4 2 ♣ A J 2

and open 1♦. The auction proceeds:

West	North	East	South
			1♦
2♣	pass	pass	?

What do you bid now?

This is obviously not a situation where partner is lurking with a trump stack, waiting for you to reopen with a takeout double which he will pass for penalties. More likely, partner has little or nothing and your clubs are badly placed. There is little future in this hand and you are well advised to pass, hoping to get a modest plus score defending 2♣. But no — one of my students, deciding that he had the clubs 'well stopped', tried 2NT and was allowed to play there. North miraculously produced a spade stopper (♠QJ63 — enormous compared with what he might have had!) but South could still take no more than his four top tricks. That was -400 against the -90 he would have conceded in 2♣ (which would have just made on the lie of the cards) — significant at any form of scoring. And after a student has had an experience like that, I find that matters get worse on the next hand when they pick up an enormous five-point hand and get another demerit for not bidding enough on it!

> *The first rule in assessing the value of a hand is to forget about absolute point-count and look at the hand in the light of what is happening around it.*

Consider the following two hands:

	a)	♠ A K Q J 10		b)	♠ A K Q 4 2
		♥ 8 6			♥ 8 6
		♦ 4 3 2			♦ J 3 2
		♣ 4 3 2			♣ J 3 2

The shapes are identical, but there are ten points on the left and eleven on the right. Yet 'expert' teachers rush to tell their students that the hand on the left is 'better'. Playing in spades, as is surely desirable, the hand guarantees five tricks while, on the right, there may only be four, even three on a bad day. That is usually considered the end of the story — but it is far from it! There is no guarantee that you will be able to buy the contract in spades and you must therefore consider your defensive prospects. All of a sudden, the hand on the right offers much greater hope. The number of spade tricks against a non-spade suit contract will vary from none to three (four is theoretically possible but most unlikely) according to the opponents' shortness in the suit. That is applicable to both hands. In the side suits, however, a couple of minor-suit queens from partner would suffice to give your side an excellent chance of two defensive tricks on the right while there may still be none on the left.

Thus the first rule of competitive bidding is to value your hand, considering all possible circumstances. You must consider the trick-taking potential of your hand according to the environment in which it will be played. There can be dramatic differences. The extreme example of a hand of thirteen clubs illustrates this perfectly. Your ten points are worth thirteen tricks if clubs are trumps, none if they are not — interesting!

Where players continually go wrong is in their failure to revalue their hand (either up or down) as the bidding progresses; mistakes of this kind, particularly in high-level competitive auctions, can cost a fortune as we shall see in the chapters to follow. A common error is to forget about the bids you have already made and to fail to assess your hand in light of them. Consider this hand — at matchpoint scoring you deal as South, with neither side vulnerable, and pick up the following:

♠ K Q 8　♥ K 8 7 4　♦ 8 6 4 3　♣ K J

You have twelve points, but there are a lot of negative features to this hand. It is aceless; most of the points are in short suits and, in particular, the club honors are unlikely to pull their full weight. The intermediates are modest — not a ten or a nine to be seen. If you do decide to open it, you're going to have to bid 1♦. This hand could hardly be worse as an opening bid and, from now on as the auction progresses, must be considered an absolute horror. On the other hand, if you take my advice and pass, then for a passed hand you could hardly be better and from now on this hand is huge! So you see that the same hand has been described as an 'absolute horror' and 'huge' within a couple of sentences. Which term applies depends on the range you have placed it in by your previous bidding.

Assessing your hand within such a range, in common bridge parlance, is referred to as the 'box' principle. Class your hand as 'good' or 'bad' according to the range in which you have set it. A fifteen point hand, for example, is good in the 11-15 range (important, for example, in Precision Club) but poor in the strong notrump 15-17 point range. Failure to grasp this leads to a large number of expensive bidding errors.

The following examples illustrate the various ways in which a hand can be devalued or revalued. Unless otherwise stated, it is matchpoint scoring and you are South with neither side vulnerable.

West	North	East	South
1♦	dbl	1♥	?

♠ J 6 3   ♥ 9 5   ♦ K Q J 10 9   ♣ J 4 2

Eight points and solid diamonds — looks like a good hand and the number of people who would bid 1NT without giving the matter a second thought is frightening. 'You have the other suits, partner, and look at my fabulous diamonds!' Fabulous? Hopeless! How on earth are you going to make seven tricks? Give partner the expected singleton diamond and this hand may not be worth a single trick. Even if he has a doubleton, West can hold up his ace once, leaving you with just one diamond trick. You would need one of those black jacks to be an entry — most unlikely when there is an opening bid sitting to your left. Also, note that even if there is by some miracle an entry to your hand, partner could easily be void of diamonds and then your suit would still not come in. Do not think that West will be stupid enough to lead his empty suit — particularly not after his partner has failed to raise.

But now look at this hand defending 1♥. Having made a take-out double of diamonds, partner should have at least three hearts and could well have four or even five. Your black jacks will fit with partner's black cards and the opponents will only have one trick in diamonds. All of a sudden, the sun is shining.

A further point: how are opponents playing that 1♥ bid? If they play it as non-forcing, as I shall recommend in the next chapter, well and good. But many pairs, as will also be explained, play the modern style of simply ignoring the double and bidding as though North had passed. In that case, if you pass, West will be obliged to bid again and move... where? On a dream day, he will rebid his diamonds on a 3-1-6-3 hand, and you will be waiting for him with the double to end all doubles. Any other new contract can only work in your favor. But bid 1NT now, particularly criminal when you have a misfit and the opponents are in a forcing situation, and you will have warned them of impending trouble *before* it is too late.

Finally, we shall do a little roll-call on points and see what we can learn. Give West a minimum for his opener, say twelve points; we have eight, totaling twenty so far. Particularly if opponents are bidding in the 'ignore the double' style, East can be credited with at least five or six, leaving partner with about fourteen at most and probably less. This leads us to a useful tip, which holds most of the time:

Waste implies worst

In a competitive auction, if you have wasted values in opponents' suit(s), it is wise to be prepared for partner to be minimum within his range. The initial double here promised upwards of about ten points. On the auction given, the lower end of the range is likely. On that basis, it is likely that the forty points are about equally shared between N-S and E-W and, with the likelihood of your hand being near or completely useless, you are better placed in defense. Again, do you see why a pass by you is so strongly recommended?

West	North	East	South
pass	1♠	pass	2♣
pass	2♥	pass	?

♠ 10 3   ♥ 6 5   ♦ K J 8 6   ♣ A Q 10 4 2

This hand came up many years ago in an early round of a national pairs event. The rest of the room looked at this hand with ten points, two tens and diamonds well stopped and bid 2NT. North had a minimum opener so 2NT became the final contract at all tables, crashing to defeat by two or three tricks when enemy cards were not well placed. I took a different view — the first job was to value the hand. In a similar way to our first example, it appeared to me to be a total write-off. Yes, we have all the suits stopped, but with all my points in the wrong place, where are the tricks coming from? To me, this is a classic example of spotting the singleton as I suggested in an earlier chapter, based on partner's rating to be 5-4-3-1. For this reason, I preferred to give simple preference to 2♠ and we became the only pair to register a plus score (saving our necks as this made the difference between elimination and qualifying).

See the difference? You are likely to make at least one extra trick in spades via a heart ruff; the opponents can only prevent this by leading spades on the go, which surely can only be to your advantage. If they do this, you are effectively playing 2NT against a very favorable defense (spade leads) while everyone else is playing it from your side after a likely heart lead through partner.

Also note, if partner does have a hand which is at the top of his range, he can still bid again over 2♠ and then you will be happy to try 3NT. It is well known that it is easier to catch up after a slight underbid than to back-pedal after stretching. If you are in doubt as to whether to make a slight underbid or overbid, prefer the underbid, keeping a little in the bank — you are less likely to get into trouble that way.

West	North	East	South
	1♥	1NT[1]	pass
pass	2♦	pass	?

1. 15-17 HCP

♠ 6 5 4 3   ♥ —   ♦ 8 6 5 4 3 2   ♣ 9 5 3

This is a dramatic example of a hand changing from valueless to a gold mine during the auction. It started off as a Yarborough with a void in partner's suit. But now a gigantic crossruff is assured and it is only a question of how high to bid. I would recommend bidding 5♦ but I would also be seriously worried about missing more! Partner should not be bidding again when sitting under a strong notrump without a good five-card suit so let's look at a couple of extreme cases. On the one hand, the full deal could be:

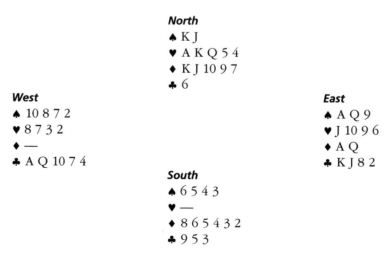

North
♠ K J
♥ A K Q 5 4
♦ K J 10 9 7
♣ 6

West
♠ 10 8 7 2
♥ 8 7 3 2
♦ —
♣ A Q 10 7 4

East
♠ A Q 9
♥ J 10 9 6
♦ A Q
♣ K J 8 2

South
♠ 6 5 4 3
♥ —
♦ 8 6 5 4 3 2
♣ 9 5 3

Here a club lead and a spade return books us for -800 and a probable bottom. But now look at this:

North
♠ A
♥ J 10 9 8 6 4
♦ A K J 9 7
♣ A

West
♠ Q 10 8 7
♥ 7 5 3 2
♦ —
♣ K J 7 4 2

East
♠ K J 9 2
♥ A K Q
♦ Q 10
♣ Q 10 8 6

South
♠ 6 5 4 3
♥ —
♦ 8 6 5 4 3 2
♣ 9 5 3

On this layout, a grand slam is absolutely solid on any lead. In the light of the notrump overcall, it is probable that East has more high cards in hearts than in diamonds and you can be confident of at least a chance for game in diamonds. But the point to note about this hand is the substantial improvement in its value after partner's diamond bid — still no points but worth at least six tricks more in a diamond contract.

West	North	East	South
			2NT
3♠	pass	pass	?

What do you bid on:

♠ A Q   ♥ K Q J 8   ♦ K J 6   ♣ K J 8 7

And you thought you had a good hand with twenty points! With the 3♠ bid sitting over you, the ♠Q is valueless, except to the extent of preventing a lead, and it is likely that at least one of your minor-suit tenaces will be badly placed. So it turns out; when this hand came up, the full deal was:

North
♠ 6 3
♥ 7 5 4 3
♦ 10 4 2
♣ Q 9 5 4

West
♠ K J 10 8 7 2
♥ A
♦ A Q 9 5 3
♣ 3

East
♠ 9 5 4
♥ 10 9 6 2
♦ 8 7
♣ A 10 6 2

South
♠ A Q
♥ K Q J 8
♦ K J 6
♣ K J 8 7

Partner can lead what he likes — your opponents are cold for 6♠, never mind 3♠! So much for your twenty points! The only question is whether East should have tried a bid over 3♠ and arguably he might, as his four points have improved markedly on the auction so far — but that is the opponents' problem. On this auction, it is likely that things are not lying well for you and you are well advised to pass, hoping perhaps for a small plus score. Note, too, that North has two points more than he might have done!

A number of further comments are appropriate here. If you advertise twenty or more points and nevertheless the opponents bid against you, then unless they are complete lunatics, it is likely that they will have tremendous distribution. Your shortage of aces is a strong warning here. Furthermore, with your partner likely to be very weak, your broken holdings in the minors are unlikely to realize their full offensive potential for lack of entries. We saw this in the first example hand shown in this chapter. Without solid holdings in your suits (like KQJ10), your hand is unlikely to realize its full potential unless partner provides some support. Therefore, facing a likely poor hand, devalue your point-count. This is something that players of most standards are very reluctant to do.

Let's take a step back for a moment, and look at the hand that makes the first overcall:

West	North	East	South
		1♦	?

Would you bid on any of these hands:

     a) ♠ K 7 3 ♥ Q J 7 5 3 ♦ 8 6 ♣ A 4 3
     b) ♠ K 7 3 ♥ Q J 7 5 3 ♦ 8 6 3 ♣ A 4
     c) ♠ K 7 3 ♥ Q J 7 5 3 ♦ 8 6 4 3 ♣ A

These are all fairly poor overcalls and the point to made here is that the hand on which you should be most reluctant to compete is (b); when sitting over a bid, the poorest holding in their suit is three small. A shortage is obviously to your advantage while length will often imply that partner has a shortage and you will be able to make some ruffs. With such a poor suit, I would be inclined to pass on all of them but the best is certainly (a) with (c) second and (b) well in the rear.

    Having seen this principle, let's go on to apply it to some more complex examples:

West	North	East	South
1♥	1♠	pass	?

    ♠ 8 ♥ K Q 10 3 ♦ K 8 6 ♣ 9 5 4 3 2

Responding to an overcall is a tricky business. The common practice of playing weak jump overcalls means that simple overcalls are very wide-ranging, possibly as good as eighteen points or so. Thus with seven points or more, you are risking missing a game if you pass. However, a more modest holding for the overcaller is likely and it is normally sensible to consider your action in that light.

    This hand is another hopeless case and yet the number opting for 1NT is alarming. Ask yourself, with little or no help for partner's spades, what this hand is worth. The heart honors are likely to be badly placed over you and, if the ♦A is also with the opening bid, you could be down to one solitary trick. Also, consider the consequences of your bid. If partner has overcalled on a weakish hand with a six-card suit, he will feel obliged to sign off in 2♠, leaving the heart lead to come through your holding and again, your hand might only be worth one or two tricks. Furthermore, East might be waiting with a crushing double.

    Now consider my recommended alternative — pass. If the contract stands, you might get away with a small penalty. Furthermore, in this day and age, most partnerships expect opener to reopen in these situations and if West does so, your prayer to defend will be answered. If West reopens with a takeout double and East does convert to penalties by passing, *then* you can think about bidding;

pass, redouble (SOS), 1NT and 2♣ (my choice) are all candidates. But the silliest thing you can do is to bid 1NT now on a totally unsuitable hand.

What about this hand on the same auction:

West	North	East	South
1♥	1♠	pass	?

♠ J 10 4   ♥ 7 5   ♦ K Q 10 3   ♣ 9 7 5 2

Here, there is a good case for a simple raise to 2♠, making it as difficult for opener to compete as possible. A straightforward raise in an overcalled suit should be considered preemptive rather than constructive. The alternative is to bid 2♦, ensuring a good lead if you eventually have to defend a club or heart contract. Practices differ in respect of how a change of suit is played opposite an overcall. Many pairs play it as a one-round force. I prefer to play it as constructive, almost certainly guaranteeing spade tolerance, but nonforcing. In this kind of situation, even if you play it as non-forcing, it is extremely unlikely in this very competitive age, that you will be left to play there. The bid has the further advantage of enabling partner to value his hand more accurately when considering whether to compete further and/or to look for game if he has a maximum overcall.

West	North	East	South
1♥	1♠	pass	?

♠ K J 9   ♥ 9 7   ♦ 9 7 6 5   ♣ J 9 7 4

This hand is ideal for a simple raise to 2♠, preempting as far as possible according to the Law of Total Tricks while showing where your values are and indicating a safe lead.

West	North	East	South
1♥	1♠	pass	?

♠ J 8 6 5   ♥ 7 5   ♦ K Q J 6 5   ♣ K 5

Here you are worth a raise to 3♠ but you should raise constructively with 3♦, forcing for one round. Partner may initially look towards 3NT but your next bid will be in spades, clarifying the position. Notice, again you ensure the correct lead should opener turn up with an enormous heart hand and buy it in 4♥.

West	North	East	South
1♥	1♠	pass	?

♠ Q J 8   ♥ A Q 7   ♦ Q 6 4   ♣ 8 6 5 4

Your eleven points have been devalued somewhat here in that the ♥Q is probably badly placed, but the spade support is excellent compensation. Now is the time to bid notrump. Note that this is recommended with a *fit* and not with a misfit, as we saw earlier. It is a close decision between 1NT and 2NT but, with the poor minor-suit holdings, I suggest that 1NT is enough. Do not make the mistake of thinking that you have to be covered in clubs as well. Hearts are the danger and you cannot be expected to look after everything. Partner should move with about fourteen points or more.

Here's an example of revaluing your hand upward:

West	North	East	South
1NT¹	2♠²	pass	?

   1.   15-17 HCP
   2.   Natural

♠ K 10   ♥ 8 5 4   ♦ Q J 10 9 6   ♣ A 3 2

This hand came up in a multiple teams' event and I bid 3♦, considered forward-going. On partner's 3♥ bid, I gave false preference to 3♠ and he bid the game, making ten tricks when the full deal proved to be:

North
♠ A Q 9 8 7 6
♥ K J 3 2
♦ K 2
♣ 9

West
♠ J 3 2
♥ A Q 9 6
♦ A 5
♣ K J 7 4

East
♠ 5 4
♥ 10 7
♦ 8 7 4 3
♣ Q 10 8 6 5

South
♠ K 10
♥ 8 5 4
♦ Q J 10 9 6
♣ A 3 2

The 'expert' sitting East commented that he would not have moved over 2♠, so an important point arises here. I took a very positive view of my hand because, sitting under the 1NT bid, I had no tenaces and therefore nothing to devalue. Likewise, my partner had broken holdings over the bid and also felt justified in valuing his hand upward. If you are sitting with solid holdings under a bid and/or broken holdings over it, you are probably justified in taking a rosy view of the position. Conversely, if you have broken holdings under a bid and/or solid holdings over it, you should probably take a more pessimistic view.

West	North	East	South
		1♥	1♠
3♥	3♠	4♥	?

Would you bid on any of these hands:

     a) ♠ A Q J 10 3 ♥ 8 ♦ K 8 6 ♣ 7 4 3 2
     b) ♠ A Q J 10 3 ♥ 8 6 ♦ K 8 6 ♣ 7 3 2
     c) ♠ A Q J 10 3 ♥ 8 6 4 ♦ K 8 6 ♣ 7 2

Here again, look at your length in the opponents' suit. Particularly if they have competed to a high — say, game — level, it is reasonable to assume that they have nine trumps between them; now the most unfavorable holding for you is a doubleton. You might therefore be keen to sacrifice on (a) and (c) but, on (b), it is probably wise to pass and let partner offer a second opinion.

West	North	East	South
2♥[1]	dbl[2]	pass	?

     1. 5-9 points, 6-card suit
     2. Takeout

What do you bid on:

     a) ♠ 10 8 ♥ A 8 6 ♦ K Q J 10 9 6 ♣ J 3
     b) ♠ 10 8 ♥ K Q ♦ Q J 10 9 6 5 ♣ A 3

You will obviously be thinking about 3NT on both hands, but the critical point here is the nature of the heart stopper. Despite the extra point in hand (b), hand (a) is a far better bet. In (a), you can, if necessary, hold up your stopper to the third round. Now only a side-suit ace in the preemptive hand is likely to defeat you. In (b), the opponents can insist that you take your heart trick on the first round, after which East is almost certain to be able to return the suit if he gets in. Also, the diamonds will probably take longer to establish. Thus 3NT is the right action on (a). On b), the decision is more difficult and the suggested approach is discussed in Chapter 7 in the section on bidding against weak two's. The point I want to make here is the difference between a flexible and an inflexible stopper for notrump.

The same principles can be applied in non-competitive auctions too:

West	North	East	South
		pass	1♥
pass	3♦¹	pass	?

1. Limit raise with four trumps

What do you bid on:

a) ♠ 8 5 ♥ A K Q 10 3 ♦ Q 8 6 ♣ J 4 3
b) ♠ A 8 6 ♥ J 10 9 8 4 ♦ K 8 6 ♣ A 3

Both hands have twelve points and 5233 shapes but the distribution of high cards is dramatically different. On hand (a), there are losers all over the place while on (b), the trumps are much poorer but there are plenty of controls. The point here is that partner's bidding has improved hand (b) to a far greater extent so that now your trumps are working overtime. In hand (a), the trumps were scoring anyway. I would pass with (a) and bid game with (b).

When supported, poor suits improve in value far more than good suits. You can overdo it in trumps: unless you are very unlucky, opposite 9 8 7 6 5, for example, A K 4 3 2 will be as effective as A K Q J 10 . Very often, those three extra points will be wasted and could be better employed elsewhere.

Points to remember

1. You must value your hand in the environment in which it will be played. Absolute point-count and distribution are little more than an initial guide. The following factors are crucial, especially in competitive auctions:
    i) Your actual point-count *within the range you have promised*,
    ii) Whether your points are in short suits (better for defense) or long suits (better for offense), remembering that by 'short' or 'long', I refer to the combined holdings *of the partnership*,
    iii) Even if you only hold small cards, length in partner's and opponents'

suits is relevant.

2. If you have wasted values in opponents' suits, especially if your high cards are placed badly under a bid, you are justified in taking a pessimistic view of the whole picture and being prepared for partner to have a minimum hand within his announced range.

3. If you are in doubt between stretching or making a slight underbid, i.e. if you feel your hand is, for example, a little too good for 2♠ but not quite strong enough for 3♠, prefer the underbid. It is usually easier to catch up than to back pedal and also life tends to be easier for partner if the level is kept low.

4. You will normally need some support from partner if your points are to realize their full trick-taking potential, especially with broken holdings. Even very big hands seldom live up to their promise facing a poor dummy. Lacking the entries to take finesses, you will lose out even if enemy cards are well-placed.

5. Broken holdings may be revalued upward when well-placed over opponents' strong hands and vice versa. Similarly, solid holdings will still pull their weight even if they are badly placed under a strong hand.

6. Poor suits increase in value far more than good suits when they are supported. You can be too strong in trumps, for example. To take an extreme case, a twelve-card suit missing the deuce is no better a holding than twelve cards missing the king!

6

Passing the buck

Points are continually lost through the mishandling of doubles, both takeout and penalty. Recently, it has become popular to rely on the Law of Total Tricks in competitive situations. Certainly the Law is a useful tool in helping you decide how high to bid in contested auctions, but remember counting trumps is no more than a rough guide. There are many factors that affect your side's trick-taking potential, including voids, extremes of distribution, secondary fits, honors in the opponents' suit, and other ifs and buts; fanatical application of the Law will rarely improve the scores of the ignorant.

We shall discuss bidding in high-level contested auctions in a later chapter, but let's start at a low level by looking at the takeout double. First of all, what does the bid mean? In principle, the doubler is showing shortness in the opponents' suit and inviting his partner to bid one of the other three. However, very strong balanced hands have to be shown by doubling and then bidding notrump. Similarly, suit-oriented hands that are too strong for a simple overcall have to begin by competing with a double.

We'll worry about responding to partner's takeout double in the next chapter. The focus here is on how opener's partner should bid after a takeout double has been made. The modern treatment is to ignore the double and bid as you would have done after a pass with the following exceptions:

1) Redouble shows about ten points or more and, for most partnerships, is penalty-oriented (although some are just showing the point-count; the extent of their fit or misfit will be shown later);

2) A bid of 2NT shows a limit raise or better in opener's suit;

3) A direct raise to three of opener's suit is preemptive and promises little more than four trumps (or five where your system allows three-card minors);

4) Many partnerships agree that a jump in a new suit is a 'fit' jump — it shows the suit bid, a fit in opener's suit and a willingness to play at least as high as the three-level; alternatively this can be played as preemptive, with a hand that looks something like a weak two-bid.

This all seems fairly sensible and is definitely easy to remember, but there is much room for improvement. The above method, in my view, misses out in one basic respect — it neglects the fact that, unless the doubler's partner is planning to pass for penalties, he has to bid something. Therefore, not only will you have a second chance to bid but both opener and the doubler may bid a second time as well, after which you will surely be far better informed as to what to do. The treatment that I'm about to describe has worked for me, virtually without mishap, over a long period of time.

There are three basic factors in valuing your hand after partner (North) has opened and East has doubled: general hand strength, length in partner's suit, and whether your high cards are placed for offense (in partner's suit) or defense (outside partner's suit).

Firstly then, we need to define 'shortness', 'intermediate length' and 'length' in partner's suit. This is another area in which many players go lamentably wrong. This is my tip:

Two's company; three's a crowd!

Shortness, in my opinion, should be defined as a singleton or void; you should be most hesitant in treating a doubleton as such. Giving partner a five-card suit, you will need a 3-3 break to benefit from a ruff if you have a doubleton, and if the suit's going to behave that well, maybe it should be your trump suit. Even if he has only four, you will need a 4-3 break to get your ruffs. The doubleton is an 'intermediate' length holding. Three or more cards should be treated as 'length'; if you have this good a fit for partner, defending a suit contract at a low level is unlikely to be very profitable.

Secondly, we must draw a line between 'weak' and 'strong' hands for responder. My view, shared by most players, is that, for the purpose of the penalty-oriented redouble, ten points or more should be considered strong enough. This should ensure an overall balance of the points to your side unless your style is to open very light. Some pairs adhere to the Rule of Nineteen for opening bids — the combined length of two longest suits plus point-count must equal or exceed nineteen. This allows them to open very distributional, low point-count hands. For reasons that are explained in an earlier chapter, I believe this to be a losing tactic in the long run.

Thirdly, we need to think about how many of our points can be in partner's suit before we have a solely offensive hand. I suggest that four or more should qualify our hand as offensive; with two or less it should be considered defensive; three is in the gray area.

As you decide what action to take over their takeout double, the first consideration is always whether you want to declare or defend. With shortness in partner's suit, you want to defend, whatever your hand strength. With length and high cards in partner's suit, you have an offensive hand. Other holdings are less clear-cut, and much will depend on how high the bidding goes. There is also a chance that you have fit in some other suit — the double has not ruled that out, it has just made it less likely.

After the double, a wide selection of actions is available: you can raise partner, bid a new suit, or bid notrump, all of these with or without jumping; you can also pass or redouble. After you pass or redouble, you will usually have the same array of bidding options when your turn comes round again, which it almost always will. Without trying very hard, we've come up with thirty or forty possible sequences. What we need to do now is to match these actions to the situations in a manner that is logical and easy to remember. So let's establish some general principles and then look at some examples to see how they are applied in practice.

1) *If you have a singleton or void in partner's suit and a weak hand, there is significant danger that West will pass and convert the double to penalties.* This is a strong possibility when partner has opened what might be a short minor suit. You should, however, always assume that opener has at least a four-card suit. Once a takeout double has been made, the probability that opener's suit is genuine increases markedly since East is known to be short; also, if opener does have only a three-card suit and the takeout double is passed for penalties, he should run or redouble for rescue.

If you have a five-card suit to bid at the one-level or a six-card or longer suit to bid at the two-level, my advice is: bid it. Note that, contrary to the 'ignore the double' approach, I play this bid as non-forcing — it has to be, since you could have a very weak hand. Indeed, it is a strong message to partner to let matters rest.

2) With a weak hand and a doubleton in partner's suit, pass and be prepared to defend. Remember, partner may bid again and you will always have the option to come back in if West bids a new suit and that gets passed round to you. Very often, West will have length in your partner's suit and bid 1NT — which you will pass or double, according to strength. You should, by now, have been cured of rushing into notrump on misfit hands. As a general rule, it is unwise to remove doubles of any kind to notrump. Of course, there are always exceptions, typically with long solid minor suits, but this is a good guide, especially at the lower levels of bidding. We'll suggest a use for the 1NT bid shortly.

If you have a doubleton in partner's suit, it is most unlikely that the double will be left in and therefore you are almost guaranteed another chance to bid if you pass now. Your first question should be 'Are we likely to be defending or declaring?'

3) With a good fit for partner (three or more trumps) and little or no defense outside, you should raise the suit as high as you dare, vulnerability obviously being an important factor. If you wish, you can also adopt the option of the 'fit' jump (a jump in a new suit showing at least a limit raise for partner and a good side suit) if all your values are in the two suits. With a singleton or void and a good hand, you can splinter. I like the following structure:

Simple raise	weak and preemptive
1NT	serious raise to the two level
jump raise	weak and preemptive; more trumps than the simple raise — raise to your Law level right away.

2NT	limit raise
jump in new suit	fit jump
double jump in new suit	splinter

Note the use of both 1NT and 2NT to show 'serious' as opposed to 'preemptive' raises.

4) With a good fit but plenty of high cards outside (i.e. you can defend if you want to), you should pass first and raise later, with or without a cuebid (few partnerships seem even to have thought of this distinction). Then, if the opponents sacrifice, partner

can take his decision as to whether to bid on or double, knowing the exact situation. Contrast this with the popular trend of raising indiscriminately, after which partner could well be on a guess as to your defensive prospects. You also have the option to pass and then jump in a suit of your own, forcing for one round and showing a willingness to play either in your suit or partner's at the cheapest level available. You promise at least five cards in your suit and at least three in partner's.

5) With a strong hand and shortness in partner's suit, redouble, intending to:

       i) Double the opponents somewhere for penalties.

or   ii) Bid a suit of your own, if you have a playing-type hand, despite the misfit.

or   iii) Cuebid if you have two suits to offer or are looking for notrump.

6) With a strong hand and intermediate length in partner's suit, then the stronger you are, the more justification there is to redouble and defend despite the 'unsatisfactory' holding in partner's suit. Vulnerability is likely to be relevant in these gray-area cases. Otherwise, pass and come back in on the next round, leaving all options still open. The cuebid is also still available.

Let's summarize this in a chart:

Fit for partner	Strength	High cards in partner's suit	Hand type	Action
0-1	weak (0-9)		unclear	run
0-1	strong (10+)		defensive	redouble
2	any	any	unclear	pass
3+	weak	yes	offensive	raise preemptively
3+	weak	no	unclear	pass
3+	strong	yes	offensive	raise constructively
3+	strong	no	unclear	pass

The main difference between what I am suggesting here and 'standard' methods is the number of hand types on which I like to pass and await events.

Give yourself as South one of your usual everyday hands:

♠ 8 6 5 4 ♥ 8 7 5 ♦ 9 6 5 ♣ 8 4 2

West, to your left, deals and opens 1♠ and partner doubles for take-out. If East passes, you are in a lamentable plight, with no sensible bid. The pressure is truly on. But if he bids, the pressure is off; admittedly a redouble might put pressure on partner but he is far better informed on what to do. I have passed enormous hands in the East position in such situations and am still counting my winnings!

Some South players panic with the above hand and pass the double, my partner rolling in anything from nine to eleven tricks for a huge result at any form of scoring. Others try 1NT, invariably raised by a strong doubler, bringing me in 800 or more. A third group select 2♣ (the correct bid, in my opinion, but hardly ideal); again, a strong doubler, under the impression that his partner has some values since he assumes that I (East) haven't, often pushes too far and I gain another enormous haul on a partscore hand. Here's another example; this time the takeout double is from the balancing seat on your right, but the principle is the same:

West	North	East	South
		pass	1♠
pass	pass	dbl	?

♠ A K J 7 5 3   ♥ K 6 2   ♦ Q 9   ♣ A K

What would you bid now, vulnerable, at matchpoints? South, deeming that he had 'underbid' on the first round, now bid 3♠ and soon found himself on the wrong end of -800 when West doubled and the full hand was:

North
♠ 4
♥ 10 5 4 3
♦ 8 7 5
♣ 9 8 7 5 3

West
♠ Q 10 6 2
♥ Q J 8
♦ A J 6 2
♣ J 10

East
♠ 9 8
♥ A 9 7
♦ K 10 4 3
♣ Q 6 4 2

South
♠ A K J 7 5 3
♥ K 6 2
♦ Q 9
♣ A K

South was wrong to bid on a number of counts. Firstly, his hand has plenty of defense and there is no need to preempt; 3♠ should be considered preemptive in this auction. Secondly, his partner now had another chance. Assuming six points as minimum for a response, then having passed 1♠, partner could make a bid now with four points or so, being 'big' in his range. If he failed to do so, it would be likely that he had nothing and that South, at best, would be good for a low partscore. Thirdly, South himself was almost certainly guaranteed another chance. The only exception would be when West passed the double of 1♠, converting it to penalties. If that was going to happen, South should not be bidding even 2♠, never mind 3♠!

If South passes, West will probably bid 1NT after which South is warned that there is trouble ahead in spades. If West has a double stopper, South had better keep quiet. If he has only one stopper, there is every chance that 1NT will go for 200. In either case, it must be right to defend and wrong to compete. It is amazing how many players find it impossible to sell out at all on twenty points at any level, never mind the one-level!

But enough chit-chat; the best way to get used to these ideas is to look at plenty of examples. We shall assume that we are playing matchpoints with neither side vulnerable but, in dubious cases, you should consider how your action might change bid if the vulnerability or method of scoring were different. In all examples, partner (North) deals and opens 1♥ and East doubles. Think about what you would bid on each of the following hands and how you would expect subsequent rounds of bidding to go.

♠ 6 5 4 3 2
♥ —
♦ Q J 4 2
♣ J 4 3 2

Bid 1♠. If you pass, there could be trouble here if West is long in hearts, while those spades may be worth a trick or two if they are trumps. Warned of your extreme shortness in hearts, partner has the option to bid a minor if he dislikes spades so you may still find a fit. Note the dilemma that the 'ignore the double' merchants are in. They either pass, risking a heavy penalty, or bid 1♠, forcing, after which partner may well rebid 2♥, leading to an even bigger penalty!

♠ 7 5 2
♥ 2
♦ J 7 6 5 4 2
♣ 9 7 6

Again, you should run, this time to 2♦; your hand is worthless unless those diamonds are trumps.

♠ 9 7 4
♥ 7 4
♦ Q J 8 5
♣ K Q 7 4

Here a pass should be preferred; the 'naturals' remove to 1NT with no spade stopper and possibly poor offensive potential, especially if partner proves to be 4-5 in spades and hearts. Let your left-hand opponent bid. If they stop in 1♠, you can always make a takeout double for the minors, willing to play in 2♥ if necessary. But the pass has another big advantage in many situations. Supposing that either opener and/or the doubler are very strong, doubler's partner is going to be in awful trouble with a very weak hand and long hearts. Give him a 2-5-3-3 Yarborough and what does he bid? I still have nightmares.

♠ 8 7 3 2
♥ 7
♦ 9 8 6 4
♣ 8 6 5 4

This time, you have the nightmare but a pass seems to be wisest, hoping partner is long in hearts and that doubler's partner cannot pass for penalties; remember that even if he does, partner still has the option to move if his hearts are weak. The bidding is not yet over and your best chance to end up defending is to pass now.

♠ K 6
♥ K J 4
♦ 10 8 4 2
♣ J 8 6 5

This hand is a good raise to 2♥ with good trumps and you should show it by bidding 1NT. Partner now has the option of making game try in either minor at the two-level!

♠ 10 9
♥ Q J 2
♦ J 4 2
♣ 9 8 6 5 3

This is a weak raise to 2♥ and you should take up as much bidding space as possible by bidding it directly.

♠ 6 3 2
♥ A Q 8 7
♦ 9 4
♣ Q 8 6 5

With four good trumps and eight points, this constitutes a poor, preemptive raise to 3♥ and you should bid it directly.

♠ Q J 4 2
♥ K Q 7 4
♦ 8 5
♣ K 9 7

Here you have a good raise to 3♥ and should show it with 2NT, forcing to at least 3♥. Partner again has room to make a game try in a minor.

♠ A K 9 6
♥ 7 4
♦ Q 9 4 2
♣ 7 5 4

Here it is not clear what is going to happen and I suggest passing for now. As the doubler is primarily looking for a fit in the other major, nothing could be less productive than to bid 1♠. Give partner a singleton and you have just saved the opponents from landing in their badly-breaking 4-4 fit. If the opponents get together in a minor, you can always come back in with a double, prepared to compete in hearts or the other minor. Note, again this is the sort of hand where doubler's partner is likely to be weak and long in hearts and he could be in awful trouble if you pass and he has to bid. I have had a long string of successes in this everyday situation. The normal 1♠, played as forcing, is likely to get you to a partscore your way with no guarantee that you will make it. I strongly recommend that you try to defend with these hands.

♠ K 7 5 2
♥ 2
♦ A K 4 2
♣ A 9 8 6

You have the opponents at your mercy and you should redouble, intending to double anything they bid.

♠ A Q J 4
♥ 9 8 7
♦ 8 5
♣ 9 7 5 3

You have a decent raise to 2♥ but with all your points outside trumps. Clarify this to partner by passing now and bidding 2♥ next time. Again, I advise against bidding spades.

♠ A K Q 8 6 5
♥ 8
♦ 9 6 4
♣ K 8 6

Here you will probably want to declare rather than defend, despite the misfit, and you should tell partner by redoubling now and then jumping in spades. Partner will probably either raise you to 4♠ or bid 3NT. If he persists with hearts, it will be in the knowledge that he can expect no more than a singleton from you. Respect his decision.

♠ K Q J 8 7
♥ 7
♦ K Q J 4 2
♣ 9 8

Here again, you will probably want to play rather than defend. I would redouble and, after a presumed 2♣ from one of the opponents, cuebid 3♣ to show this type of hand. 3NT or game in one of your suits will probably be the final contract. Let partner decide.

♠ K 5 2
♥ 2
♦ A K Q J 8 7 2
♣ 9 7

Here 3NT is a favorite to be the final contract, but why rush? There is no law against clubs being wide open, while anything up to 7♦ could be making. Redouble first and then bid 3NT if opponents bid spades, or 3♦ if they bid clubs. Partner will then be well placed to choose the final contract.

♠ A J 9 4
♥ K
♦ 8 5 4
♣ K 8 6 5 2

Here again, you will redouble first, intending to double either black suit. If opponents run to 2♦, you can now bid 2♥! This is a very rare situation where you redouble and then later support partner — where your singleton is one of the two top honors. Your failure to double 2♦ will indicate precisely this type of hand.

♠ 6 3 2
♥ 9 8 7
♦ K 6
♣ A K Q 8 7

This is a playing rather than a defensive type of hand but, with twelve points in side suits, there is plenty of defensive potential and no need to fear that opponents can make anything. I recommend that you pass and then jump to 3♣ over a likely removal to 1♠. This is forcing and shows clubs and a willingness to play 3♥. Again, note the possibility that doubler's partner has a weak 3-5-3-2, when he might elect to sit for the double rather than mislead partner by bidding a non-existent major. It has happened countless times. And if he does bid 1♠ on a three-bagger, the doubler could choose to sacrifice against 4♥, especially at favorable vulnerability (remember he will be void in hearts), resulting in a dreadful penalty when 4♥ was not making — a huge loss. Notice also that the 'ignore the double' merchants' natural and forcing 2♣ takes the pressure off the doubler's partner again here, the last thing you want.

I could go on almost indefinitely but this should be enough to show how the structure works and how accurate it is. In order to ensure that you understand the method completely, we must now return to the opener and look at how he rebids after a takeout double when partner has chosen his action from the array of possibilities above. To cover them all would require far more space than we want to use up here, so we'll just look at a few typical situations to make sure you get the idea. In each case, assume neither side is vulnerable at matchpoints.

West	North	East	South
			1♥
dbl	2♣	various	?

♠ K 8 7   ♥ A K Q J 9   ♦ 6 5 3 2   ♣ 4

Your rebid problem is going to vary, of course, depending on what action, if any, East takes. However, it is important to remember that partner has a singleton or void in hearts and is almost certainly long in clubs. If he wanted you to return to 2♥, he would not have taken you out of 1♥ doubled — a point that most players miss. Note also how much easier it is to value your hand in light of this.

If East passes, you have three options: pass, 2♦ and 2♥ (despite the misfit); I like a pass. If you bid again you advertise the fact that the hand is a misfit, merely inviting trouble. West may well compete in one of the other suits, after which you will be delighted to defend. Incidentally, with a much better hand you are allowed to raise clubs, should you have a fit for partner.

If East doubles 2♣ for penalties (which he should not do unless he is prepared to double 2♥ as well), you have a different problem. Bidding 2♦ is likely to land you in worse trouble and the hand is likely to be worth more with clubs, rather than hearts, as trumps. You will probably be able to contribute tricks with those heart honors even if clubs are trumps while partner's long and probably poor clubs will contribute nothing if hearts are trumps. Pass and take your medicine — maybe West will pull the double!

If East takes any other action, you are content to pass and await events. Partner is weak and your side has no fit, so this is a hand to defend, not to declare.

West	North	East	South
			1♥
dbl	redbl	various	?

♠ K 8 7   ♥ A Q J 9 6   ♦ Q 5 3 2   ♣ Q

Again partner has shown a heart singleton or void and a likely desire to defend. If East passes, you have nothing to say. Let West try to rescue himself and partner will take things from there. If East bids over the redouble, you should double spades or diamonds, and pass 2♣ around to partner for a decision.

That's not to say that you should always defend once partner has redoubled. Holding this:

♠ A 9 4   ♥ A 10 7 4 2   ♦ —   ♣ K Q J 10 8

you would have little interest in defending a diamond contract; meanwhile there could be anything up to a slam on in clubs. This is not a time to leave things to partner — bid 3♣ whatever East does, and make the position clear. At worst, you will probably end up in 3NT with good prospects.

West	North	East	South
			1♥
dbl	pass	1♠	pass
pass	2♣	pass	?

Much depends on your exact hand here so we'll look at three different examples. Remember, by passing over the double partner has promised a minimum of a doubleton heart and you should choose your contract accordingly.

♠ K 8 7
♥ A Q J 9 6
♦ Q 5 3 2
♣ J

Partner cannot have four diamonds — he would have balanced with a double with three alternative contracts to offer. Just sign off in 2♥.

♠ A 2
♥ Q J 6 5 2
♦ A J 4 2
♣ Q 7

Here you probably have a 5-2 fit in both suits and, at matchpoints, it is probably right to bid 2♥ again. At teams, passing 2♣ should be preferred as it's safer, and the scoring advantage of a major over a minor less important than securing a plus. Partner may have six clubs and, even if he doesn't, his is the weaker hand and those clubs may not be of any use unless they are trumps.

♠ Q J 4 3
♥ A Q J 4 2
♦ Q
♣ K 9 7

This time partner could well have a singleton spade and 5♣ or even 4♥ or could be on. It is worth making a try for game by raising to 3♣.

This chapter has certainly been a lot of hard work, but the effort was surely worth it for such an increase in accuracy. Try it out with your favorite partner — I guarantee you won't go back to 'standard' methods!

Points to remember

1. Note, all the way through, how insistent I am on distinguishing between ability to play and ability to defend. Above all, one of my most important tips is that, if opponents are in a forcing situation and you are able to defend, let them bid. Over my bridge career, this tactic has brought me in more points than most other bidding tips put together. It is alarming how many players are obsessed with the idea that it is bidding, rather than passing, which puts pressure on opponents — in a forcing situation, exactly the opposite is true. The situation after a takeout double is a classic example.

2. Standard 'ignore the opponents' methods are less descriptive than they could be; they also take the pressure off the opponents unnecessarily. Consider playing my suggested structure, and start collecting more juicy penalties!

7

Double jeopardy

Let's turn our attention now to bidding when partner has made a takeout double and the next hand has taken one of its various possible actions. It needs to be emphasized that very few players use the methods I recommended in the last chapter for countering a takeout double, so most will not pass that often in this auction. Therefore, you as doubler's partner, will have to be prepared to cater to a whole host of possible intervening bids.

Again, you have a distressingly large number of possible actions available. Over a pass you can bid a suit or notrump, with or without jumping, you can pass for penalties, and you can cuebid. Over a bid, you have a second cuebid available as well as a double. Again, I shall try to establish some general principles rather than attempt to cover every possible situation.

The first task is to specify meanings for your possible actions; but even more importantly, to decide whether bids are sign-off, invitational or forcing. In many areas there are disagreements, even among experts, so what follows must only be considered my recommendation rather than something that is categorically right or wrong. However, you will (I hope!) agree that my approach is logical and quite easy to remember. As always, it is crucial to have some kind of agreement within your partnership; whether your system is theoretically the best is of lesser importance.

W	N	E	S
1♥	dbl	pass	?

My basic guide is this: *since the opponents have bid a suit, a cuebid is available and that should be the only forcing bid.* Therefore in this auction your only forcing bid is 2♥ which simply asks partner to describe his hand further. It is forcing to a notrump bid (always limited) or suit agreement; in other words, if the doubler bids a suit below game level, the cuebidder guarantees to bid again (although most partnerships allow the cuebidder to pass if he is a passed hand). This force continues until a suit has been agreed or game is reached, or until the doubler makes a limited notrump bid.

W	N	E	S
1♥	dbl	pass	3♦

All bids in response to the double other than the cuebid are non-forcing. Many players find this difficult to understand, since they believe that a jump in a new suit is forcing. The fallacy here is to consider those diamonds as a 'new' suit. They are not — the doubler bid them along with spades and clubs when he made his takeout double. Thus the 3♦ bid is merely showing support. Even a jump to 4♦ should be played as non-forcing. So the doubler's partner should normally bid his hand to the limit with his first bid. If he has two suits, or does not know what to do for some other reason, he cuebids and bidding continues until a fit is found, or until a game or a notrump contract is reached.

W	N	E	S
1♦	dbl	1♥	?

The next problem is to agree on what to do if opener's partner bids a new suit over the double so that cuebids in two suits become available. *My suggestion here is to use the cuebids as dual purpose: to show both the other suits and to search for notrump.* In that case, 2♥ would advertise a good heart stopper but an inability to stop diamonds, and vice versa for 2♦. The cuebidder must, of course, be prepared to play in at least one of the black suits should partner fail to provide the necessary stopper in the other suit.

W	N	E	S
1♥	dbl	2♥	?

After a direct raise, a double is usually played as responsive, throwing the choice back to the doubler, typically on a 3-2-4-4 hand, willing to play at the three-level or higher. Responsive doubles are normally played up to and including 4♦.

W	**N**	**E**	**S**
1♥	dbl	2♦	dbl

Double of a new suit bid by East is different; I strongly advise you to play this double as penalties. But you must have travanced action on an escape to 2♥.

Now we have to agree approximate point ranges for the various new-suit and notrump responses. Obviously, distribution needs to be taken into account as well as whether or not responder's points are 'working' — in this auction you would discount heart honors which are likely to be badly placed and facing shortness. Obviously, though, the ♥A will still be worth a trick but lower honors are of much more dubious value. My suggestion is as follows:

Simple change of suit	0-7 working points
Jump change of suit	8-10 working points at the two-level; 9-11 working points at the three-level

You should tend to value your hand more optimistically if you are bidding a major, where you are very likely to get support (it is a major-suit fit, after all, that the doubler is usually seeking). However, you should hold back with a minor suit, where the doubler need not be so strong and you would, anyway, need eleven tricks for game — much less likely when the opposition have opened the bidding. For a move to notrump, I suggest 8-10 for 1NT and 11-13 for 2NT; with more, just bid game.

Remember that you are probably bidding with a misfit and with points badly placed in opener's suit. Unless there are long running suits around and/or strong intermediates, it is unlikely that you will make game with less than twenty-six points between you, even with the advantage of knowing the location of most, if not all, of the enemy strength. Let's look at some examples emphasizing positions where players continually go astray. Again, we shall assume neither side vulnerable at matchpoint scoring.

W	**N**	**E**	**S**
1♦	dbl	pass	?

♠ 9 7
♥ 9 7 6 4
♦ K Q 3 2
♣ 8 5

You have been asked to choose your best non-diamond suit and there should be no problem here: bid 1♥. Do not be tempted to bid 1NT; firstly, you are nowhere near strong enough; secondly, even if you were, that diamond holding may only be worth one stopper. This hand is hopeless and the lower the bidding is kept, the better.

W	N	E	S
1♦	dbl	pass	?

♠ 7 2
♥ J 7 5 2
♦ A Q J 4 2
♣ 9 8

The diamonds here are certainly a considerable improvement over our first hand but I still strongly recommend that you stick to bidding 1♥. Partner is probably something like 4-4-1-4 and 1NT is the last thing he wants to hear, especially if he has stretched to double on a shapely eleven points (some players do it on even less!). Note a further point overlooked even by good players. If you bid 1♥, you are promising nothing, and a fairly strong West might feel entitled to compete, after which you will be thrilled to defend. Bid 1NT, however, and you are warning opponents of the diamond stack and will almost certainly persuade them that it is better not to compete.

At matchpoints, when opponents are vulnerable, it is worth considering a pass, trying to collect the magic +200. In my experience, this will work occasionally but in the long term, is ill-advised. You have no entries outside the diamond suit and will be unable to draw declarer's trumps easily; you will too often concede -140 or even -240 or -340.

W	N	E	S
1♦	dbl	pass	?

♠ A J 4 3
♥ A 9 7 4 2
♦ Q
♣ 7 6 4

Here, with nine working points and a double fit, game in a major may well be on. It is best to start with a cuebid of 2♦, making it clear to partner that, at the moment, you are not sure where to play. Partner will probably choose a major and you will raise to the three-level (invitational now that a suit has been agreed). Partner will choose the final contract from there.

W	N	E	S
1♦	dbl	pass	?

♠ 5 4 2
♥ 8 7 5
♦ Q J 8 4
♣ 9 5 3

This one is a real nightmare. The first point, and this applies to all such situations in bridge, is: 'Keep your head!' More points are lost through ignoring this than through any lack of bridge skill. The second point to note is that partner has forced you to speak. If you pass in this sequence, that is a *strong* bid. The same applies to 1NT, so both are ruled out. All you can do is bid the cheapest suit available, 1♥; you promise no more than you have. How nice it would have been had East made a bid! When you get into a desperate situation, aim to minimize the damage.

W	N	E	S
1♦	dbl	pass	?

♠ J 10 8 7 6
♥ 9 7
♦ K J 3 2
♣ A 4

Clearly you will bid your spades now, but how many is right? The fifth spade is certainly worth something but your diamond holding could hardly be worse. You are close to a jump with five working points (ignore those diamond cards!) but you should probably take the view that game is unlikely if partner cannot move over 1♠. But remember that for a 1♠ bid your hand is huge — one move from partner should rocket you into 3NT or more likely, 4♠.

W	N	E	S
1♦	dbl	pass	?

♠ 7 6 2
♥ 5 2
♦ A J 4 2
♣ 10 9 8 5

Another nightmare, particularly as partner is primarily looking for majors. But again, you have to answer. Pass and 1NT are ruled out for reasons discussed earlier. On an earlier hand you were forced into bidding a three-card major for lack of something better. You already know my opinion about lying in major suits. Here it is unnecessary and you should simply bid 2♣.

W	N	E	S
1♦	dbl	pass	?

♠ A 5 4 2
♥ 7 5
♦ 8 4
♣ A K 9 5 3

Here it is unclear how high and in which suit the bidding will go and you should inform partner of this with a cuebid of 2♦. After a likely 2♥, you will bid 3♣, showing this type of hand. Remember that this is forcing, since no suit has yet been agreed, so if you have a spade fit it will never be missed. Note that also, on a lucky day when partner bids 2♠ first time, you still have the option to bid 3♣, still forcing, before raising spades — it might help a slam-minded partner. He does not have to have more than an uninteresting sixteen- count, say ♠ K Q 9 8 6 ♥ K Q 4 2 ♦ A 3 ♣ Q 6, for a slam to be excellent.

W	N	E	S
1♦	dbl	1♠	?

♠ J 9 7 6 4
♥ J 6 4
♦ K J 8
♣ 5 4

This time, East bids 1♠, which we'll assume does not necessarily show the intense dislike of diamonds that I insist on. It may seem tempting to double for penalties but how are you going to deal with a run-out to 2♦? Your honors are poorly placed and you have little to offer to the defense.

Notrump will not be much fun either with both spades and diamonds likely to be badly placed for you. It is best to keep quiet and pass. If your strength is in the enemy suit, prefer to defend than declare. This is one of the most widely neglected tips; many people (and not only weaker players) prefer to fly into notrump on misfit hands rather than allow their opponents to get into trouble.

W	N	E	S
1♦	dbl	1♠	?

♠ 7 2
♥ 8 5
♦ A Q 4 2
♣ A Q J 9 8

This hand is a very different matter because now you have both entries and playing strength. You are surely strong enough to play at least 2NT and you can either bid it outright, crediting partner with a good spade holding for his double, or preferably, in my opinion, bid 2♦ to show that you are well covered in diamonds but are terrified of spades. Either partner will then bid notrump himself or you will finish in a club contract. Again, the cuebid commits you to notrump, game or suit agreement.

W	N	E	S
1♦	dbl	1♠	?

♠ K J 2
♥ 8 7 5
♦ K J 8 4
♣ 9 3 2

This is another one where players would be standing in line to make a 1NT bid but where you are far better off defending; a pass is greatly preferable. The bidding is not over yet anyway.

W	N	E	S
1♦	dbl	1♠	?

♠ A Q 8
♥ 8 4 2
♦ K J 6 5
♣ 9 6 4

This is a great temptation for the notrump merchants. However, as long as 1♠ by RHO is forcing, the right action is to pass and see what happens. If the opponents die in 2♦, you can still compete in notrump although it is probably wiser to pass and defend — this hand has little offensive power but plenty of defensive strength.

W	N	E	S
1♠	dbl	2♠	?

♠ 9 7
♥ 8 6 4
♦ K Q J 10 2
♣ 5 4 2

Let's assume that East's raise is 'noise' and bid accordingly. Here you were not worth 3♦ if East had passed, but you are under pressure in this auction and are entitled to bid it now. The general guide here is that you should be prepared to be pushed up one level but no more.

W	N	E	S
1♠	dbl	2♠	?

♠ 7 2
♥ 8 5
♦ A K Q J
♣ 8 7 6 4 3

Many partnerships play 2NT as takeout for the minors in this auction, and I strongly recommend this method. The number of occasions when you will want to bid a natural 2NT is very small. If you don't play this however, you should make a responsive double, intending to correct 3♥ to 4♣ to show this hand. Any other approach creates problems and much depends on the goal you have in mind. If you believe that you will eventually be defending a spade contract, a diamond bid is vital to ensure the correct lead. However, if you anticipate buying it in one of the minors, it may be crucial to bid clubs first, then diamonds so that partner gives preference correctly.

W	N	E	S
1♠	dbl	2♠	?

♠ Q 9 8
♥ 8 6 4 2
♦ 7
♣ A K J 6 4

If partner has really good hearts and relatively little in diamonds, game in hearts could be on, but clubs could be the safer partscore. There are a number of possible approaches. One is to bid a direct 3♣, hoping that the opponents will not compete any further; if partner now bids 3♦, you can correct to 3♥, describing the hand perfectly. But if opponents compete to 3♠, are you good enough to bid 4♥? A second option is a responsive double, intending to correct diamonds to hearts. That should show this type of hand — with five or more hearts, you would have bid them directly. A third alternative is an immediate 3♥. Much depends on how confident you are that partner has four hearts; a responsive double is probably the best choice.

Points to remember

1. If the opponents have bid a suit, play the cuebid as the only forcing bid. It is forcing to suit agreement, notrump or a game contract.
2. Play responsive doubles up to and including 4♦.
3. Responder counts only 'working' points — not those in the enemy suit.
4. Be reluctant to bid notrump: remember that you are probably bidding with a misfit and with points badly placed in opener's suit. If your strength is in the enemy suit, prefer to defend than declare.
5. Revalue your hand optimistically if you are bidding a major in response to a takeout double; hold back a little with a minor suit, where the doubler need not be so strong and you would need eleven tricks for game.
6. Double them for penalties only if you can handle the likely run-out.

The reopening double

The use of negative doubles is almost universal in duplicate bridge nowadays. As a result, a direct penalty double of an overcall is not usually available to you. Instead, you have to pass (without obvious hesitation!) and hope that your partner can reopen with a takeout double which you can convert for penalties by passing. This usually works reasonably well in practice but the opening bidder must be careful with hands unsuitable for that reopening double. Here are some examples. In each case, you deal with neither side vulnerable and partner could be lurking with a heart stack:

W	N	E	S
			1♠
2♥	pass	pass	?

♠ A K 9 7 6 2
♥ 8
♦ Q J 10
♣ A 4 2

Here you have a hand which can play in either minor if partner dislikes spades and, with three top tricks in defense, can defend 2♥. It is therefore highly suitable for a balancing takeout double.

W	N	E	S
			1♠
2♥	pass	pass	?

♠ A Q J 7 6 2
♥ 8 5
♦ K J
♣ 8 7 6

This hand is less clear. Even if partner dislikes spades, your suit could be worth up to five tricks on offense while its defensive value is minimal. Furthermore, you may have little defense if opponents run to a minor. Compete with 2♠ rather than a double.

W	N	E	S
			1♠
2♥	pass	pass	?

♠ A Q J 9 8
♥ K 6 4
♦ A 8 7
♣ J 6

Yes, you have fifteen points but also both length and a dubious value in hearts, so the bidding has devalued your hand markedly. Partner has proved unable to support spades and is unlikely to be sitting with a heart stack. Even if he is, the opponents may have an excellent contract in a minor. A pass is probably prudent.

W	N	E	S
			1♠
2♥	pass	pass	?

♠ A J 9 7 5 2
♥ 9
♦ A
♣ A Q 8 5 2

This hand certainly has some defense but is still far more of a playing hand. Only in the case where partner has a heart stack and length in diamonds will it prove right to reopen with a double. In a recent Macallan Invitational Pairs with four world-class players at the table, this hand elected to reopen with a double:

North
♠ 10 3
♥ A Q 8 7 2
♦ K 4
♣ K J 6 4

West
♠ K Q 6
♥ K J 10 5 4 3
♦ 10 9 8 2
♣ —

East
♠ 8 4
♥ 6
♦ Q J 7 6 5 3
♣ 10 9 7 3

South
♠ A J 9 7 5 2
♥ 9
♦ A
♣ A Q 8 5 2

Partner did pass the double but East rescued to 3♦. This was passed round to North who, under the impression that his partner had a 'takeout double of hearts' and therefore diamond length, doubled again. The defenders were able to draw two rounds of trumps but could not prevent East from taking four diamonds, two ruffs, two spades and a heart for nine tricks and +470 while North-South were cold for 6♣ with careful play — an enormous swing. It's clear that South would have been better to reopen with 3♣. At least that would have led to a plus score even if they didn't get to the slam.

W	N	E	S
			1♠
2♥	pass	pass	?

♠ K Q J 10 7
♥ 8
♦ K Q J 10 2
♣ 5 4

Again, partner could be waiting with a heart stack but this hand, with two aceless solid suits, is very offensive and could be hopeless on defense. A reopening double should not even be considered. As in the previous example, even if partner has a heart stack, opponents could be well-placed in clubs; if they run to 3♣ you will be sitting there wondering whether you want to defend even if partner does find a double.

The question now really is whether you should just compete with 2♠ or show your diamonds at the three-level, implying a hand stronger than your actual twelve points. With such good trick-taking potential, you should probably go for 3♦.

W	N	E	S
			1♠
2♥	pass	pass	?

♠ A J 7 3 2
♥ 8 7 5
♦ A
♣ A 7 6

It is most unlikely that partner is waiting with heart stack, because of your length; nor could he scrape up a spade raise. The hand is likely to be hopeless and you should pass.

W	N	E	S
			1♠
2♥	pass	pass	?

♠ A Q 9 8 7
♥ K J
♦ 7
♣ A K J 6 4

Your eighteen points have been devalued somewhat by the heart bid, but you still have quite a good hand and a club contract or even 3NT could still be on. However, if you reopen with a double, partner is likely to bid diamonds, driving the bidding too high. With this two-suiter, bid a straightforward 3♣. Some players would be tempted to try 2NT but the heart stopper can be knocked out quickly and it is unlikely that you can run the required number of tricks in time. A trump contract will play better.

W	N	E	S
			1♠
2♥	pass	pass	?

♠ K J 8 6 2
♥ 8 7 5
♦ A K 8 4 3
♣ —

Again, partner is unlikely to have a heart stack and you should be terrified that he has a weak hand with a lot of clubs. The whole hand is probably a misfit and you should pass. Yes, you will occasionally miss a diamond partscore but you will also avoid a whole range of disasters which are likely to occur if you reopen. Note, that if partner does have a heart stack, you will probably collect a large undoubled penalty when opponents could be cold for a big club contract — not a bad result!

Once again, the important tip to pick up from these examples is that you should not try to defend — and this particularly applies at a low level — with hands more suitable for declaring. It is strange that the macho players, to whom reference has been made several times already, are very often the worst offenders in this respect. They insist on declaring most of the time but, on the very occasions when they ought to be so insistent, they go off the rails — one of the bridge world's great paradoxes!

Points to remember

1. Don't be afraid to pass out even a fairly good hand in high-card strength if it's clear from the auction that partner is weak and has no fit for you.
2. Even with shortness in the overcalled suit, be wary of a balancing double if you have good playing strength in the other suits — an offensive hand. It may well be right for you to play the hand even if partner does have a trump stack in their suit.

You can't be perfect over preempts

We have looked at takeout doubles at the one level at some length, let's turn now to auctions involving doubles of weak two-bids and higher preemptive bids. Many of the same principles will apply.

The first point is that considerable bidding space has been lost and, as there often isn't room to investigate partner's exact strength, you are going to have to make a reasonable assumption about the lie of the land. Suppose we credit the preemptor with about seven points, a suit that looks like KQxxxx at the two-level (and perhaps a seventh card in his suit at the three-level), and one high card outside his suit. Suppose your hand is a good opening bid — perhaps fifteen or sixteen points. That leaves about seventeen points unaccounted for. Sharing these equitably between the other two players gives partner about eight or nine. A reasonable conservative assumption will be about eight points so we can immediately formulate our first tip:

Assume eight at the starting gate

Your partner, bidding over the preempt, is going to assume that you have about eight points. You, therefore, should not jump or take any other action towards game or slam unless you have at least ten useful points. As usual, points in the preemptor's suit other than the ace will normally be of little worth except possibly to act as stoppers at notrump.

Bearing this in mind, there are a number of approaches. Over three-level preempts, most experts agree that the best method is to play double for takeout in both positions (immediate and balancing) against preempts at all levels, saving as much bidding space as possible while leaving the option of conversion to penalties open. This sacrifices the direct penalty double and, where the player sitting over the bid has a genuine penalty double, he is forced to pass, hoping that his partner can reopen with a double. The disadvantage of this is that the reopening double becomes very wide-ranging.

With preempts becoming more and more frivolous nowadays (as was mentioned earlier, some players preempt on pathetic five-card suits at favorable vulnerability), the case for playing the double for penalties is becoming stronger. Some pairs compromise by playing a method called **FOXU** (**F**ishbein — next suit up for takeout and double for penalties — when sitting **O**ver the bid but double (**X**) for takeout when sitting **U**nder the bid) and this works fairly well, the disadvantage being the loss of the bid of the next suit up as a natural overcall. Over weak two-bids, there is more room. Most pairs stick to the takeout double, but there are a number of other approaches, especially against weak two-bids in the majors. One alternative involves a penalty double in the immediate position, while 3♣ is used as a weak takeout double and 3♦ as a strong takeout double, drawing the line at about the sixteen-point mark.

With preempts at the four-level and higher, the general approach is to play the double as showing general values — partner is expected to pass unless he has a obvious playable contract. On hands where you definitely want to declare rather than defend, the cheapest notrump bid available is for takeout.

While these methods deal fairly well with three-suited hands and trump stacks, problems arise with two-suiters, especially 5-4 hands where the long suit is a minor. Assuming that you have agreed that double is for takeout, think about how would you bid on the following hands when sitting over a 3♦ preempt.

W	N	E	S
		3♦	?

♠ 6 4
♥ A K 8 6
♦ 6 4
♣ A K Q 3 2

There are three possible approaches. One is to double, keeping open the option of playing 3NT and being prepared to correct 3♠ to 4♣ to show this hand. However, there is the risk of finding partner with a good hand with spades and, after he bids 4♠, you will sit there wondering whether he has bid it on length in the suit, in which case it will be a playable contract, or whether he is assuming you have spades, in which case it will probably be ludicrous.

A second approach is to bid 3♥, keeping the 3NT option open; if partner bids spades now, usually played as invitational unless agreed otherwise, he will have at least a five-card suit and you can pass. The dangers are obvious though. If partner passes you may be in a very silly contract, and there is also the risk that he will credit you with five or more hearts and raise on three small, risking a bad split, a double and a heavy penalty.

A third approach is to bid 4♣, which seems the worst as 3NT is now lost (although 4NT now from partner should, in my opinion, be played as natural). Also, partner will be reluctant to introduce a four-card heart suit at this level and the best contract could be lost.

Of the three evils, you should probably prefer to double, prepared to sit for 4♠ but possibly removing it to 5♣ if you are doubled.

W	N	E	S
		3♦	?

♠ A K 8 6
♥ A K 6 4 3 2
♦ 7 4
♣ 7

Here again, there are three approaches. A double, followed by correcting 4♣ to 4♥, would show the hand admirably. But you must travance on what you are going to do if partner bids 3NT over your double. I think you should still correct to 4♥ but it could easily be wrong. A direct 4♥, instead of double, is reasonable but risks missing a spade fit, crucial if partner has length in spades and very short hearts. Nevertheless, on this kind of hand where suits are unlikely to break kindly, a 6-2 heart fit may well play better than a 4-4 spade fit. The pessimist will just overcall 3♥ in the first place, risking missing a spade fit and/or game. I prefer the first approach — the double.

W	N	E	S
		3♦	?

♠ A K 7 5 3
♥ A K 6 4 2
♦ 8 4 3
♣ —

The best way to show a major two-suiter is through a direct cuebid of 4♦. This cuts out the club suit and partner should get the message.

W	N	E	S
	3♦	?	

♠ K Q J 7 4
♥ —
♦ 6 3
♣ A K J 6 4 2

There is certainly plenty of distribution around this table, and a simple 4♣ is unlikely to be the end of the auction. Double is too dangerous with a heart void — partner is entitled to expect at least tolerance. Bid spades at your next turn and partner will be able to place the final contract.

You have probably realized that I am leading up to my next tip — that it is more important to find the correct suit than to worry about playing in game or slam. I believe it is more important to avoid large penalties, conceded through playing in the wrong suit, than to lose sleep over whether you are being talked out of a slam (which may be going down because of bad splits anyway). For that reason, on hearing a takeout double, partner should beware of going flying unless he has a suit which stands up on its own, in case the shape of the doubler's hand is less than perfect.

With this in mind, let's cross the table to become the responding hand:

W	N	E	S
3♦	dbl	pass	?

♠ K J 6 4
♥ 8 6
♦ 6 4
♣ J 9 8 3 2

A takeout double of a minor should be primarily oriented towards the majors and, as you have only six points, you should keep the bidding low with 3♠. If 3♠ is doubled for penalties, you can run to 4♣ but there has to be a two-trick advantage for that to be worthwhile. Let partner decide.

W	N	E	S
3♦	dbl	pass	?

♠ 8 6 4 3
♥ A Q 7 5
♦ 9 4
♣ A J 4

On this hand, you want to be in game in a major but you are not sure which one. Cuebid 4♦ and pass partner's reply.

W	N	E	S
3♦	dbl	pass	?

♠ K J 6 4
♥ 8 6
♦ K J 4
♣ Q 8 3 2

Here you have ten points but four of them are badly placed. There are plenty of hands where 3NT will be made, notably where the preemptor's partner has a singleton diamond, but you should devalue and settle for 3♠. Partner still has another bid and you could reach a successful 4♠.

W	N	E	S
3♦	dbl	pass	?

♠ J 6 4 2
♥ A
♦ A J 10 4
♣ Q 7 6 4

You have enough points to insist on game here and 3NT is probably the right place if you want to declare this hand. There is no guarantee that partner has four spades and certainly yours are fairly anemic. Even if you have a spade fit, your diamonds are strong enough to withstand attack and there is no guarantee that a suit contract will provide two extra tricks. The alternative action, however, which you should consider very attractive, is to pass the double. Vulnerability and method of scoring may be relevant here. At adverse vulnerability at pairs, 3NT may be preferable as the preemptor may be able to scrape six tricks in diamonds and get out for 500 against your probable 630. At other vulnerabilities, passing the double should ensure a healthy plus.

W	N	E	S
3♦	dbl	pass	?

♠ 9 6 3
♥ Q 9
♦ A 8 4 2
♣ 6 5 4 2

This hand came up in a recent major tournament. At IMP scoring and unfavorable vulnerability, a well-known expert opted to bid 3NT. Surely, if 3NT is going to make, then 3♦ doubled is likely to go for a large penalty and, at worst, the loss will be modest. This was the whole hand:

North
♠ A J 8 7
♥ J 8 6 2
♦ K 10
♣ A Q 3

West
♠ Q 5
♥ 7 5 4
♦ Q J 7 6 5 3
♣ 10 8

East
♠ K 10 4 2
♥ A K 10 3
♦ 9
♣ K J 9 7

South
♠ 9 6 3
♥ Q 9
♦ A 8 4 2
♣ 6 5 4 2

East greeted 3NT with a crushing double, whereupon South 'escaped' to 4♣, doubled again for five down and -1400. 3♦ doubled cannot be made and even if it could, -470 would have been

peanuts compared with the actual loss. One only has to give partner a couple of ace-kings to beat 3♦ while, even now, there are
only five or six tricks in notrump South showed an alarming lack of
appreciation of the position. Frankly, if South feels that a pass is out
of the question I would rate 3♠ at least as good as 3NT or 4♣. That
is likely to escape for -800 at worst.

Points to remember
1. **You can't be perfect over preempts.** You have less room to ma-
   neuver over higher level preempts, so some accuracy in bidding will in-
   evitably disappear. It is more important to find the correct suit than to
   worry about playing in game or slam.
2. Consider passing partner's takeout double for penalties instead of bidding notrump. It may well be that if you can make 3NT, the penalty
   will be worth more.

Lebensohl over doubles of weak two-bids

We are now going to look specifically at competing over weak two-
bids and introduce a useful convention which will be new to some
readers. Some partnerships play weak two-bids in all four suits,
others in all non-club suits. The majority, however, confine the ac-
tivity to the majors and, assuming you have agreed to play takeout
doubles over weak two-bids, we shall use our 'eight at the starting
gate' rule to refine our bidding.

After an opening bid of 2♥ or 2♠ has been doubled for takeout,
if the next hand passes you have similar options to those available
at the one-level. However, you have much less bidding space to
work with. With one exception, a jump shift in a new suit will involve going to the four-level which may be too high and, even more
important, rules out 3NT as final contract. To get around this problem, many players give up 2NT as a natural bid and use it conventionally to indicate a weak hand (this convention is called Lebensohl).
Over 2NT, the doubler is expected to bid 3♣, which responder will
pass or correct to the suit where he wishes to play. You can then
play a simple bid of a new suit in response to the double as showing eight working points minimum, and save jumps and cuebids
for much stronger hands. Thus, after:

	West	**North**	**East**	**South**
	2♠	dbl	pass	?

with a hand like:

♠ 8 6   ♥ K J 7 5 3   ♦ 8 5 3   ♣ J 7 4

you will bid 2NT, and, on hearing the obligatory 3♣, bid 3♥ which is a sign off. With a hand like:

♠ 8 6   ♥ A K 9 5 3   ♦ 8 5 3   ♣ J 7 4

on the same auction, you have enough to suggest a game and you bid a direct 3♥, showing about 8-10 points, but still non-forcing. The only disadvantage of this method is that the natural 2NT bid, which you would want to use with a balanced 9-10 points and a good (preferably double) stopper in the preemptor's suit, has been lost. When you have this hand, you now have to choose between sitting for the double and shooting 3NT. Vulnerability, method of scoring and the quality of your holding in the preemptor's suit will all be relevant.

Some example hands will make the value of the Lebensohl method clear.

W	**N**	**E**	**S**
2♠	dbl	pass	?

♠ J 6
♥ J 8 6
♦ J 9 8 3 2
♣ 6 4 3

This is a very poor hand and you just want to get out in 3♦. Therefore use the Lebensohl forcing 2NT and bid 3♦ over partner's enforced 3♣ response.

W	**N**	**E**	**S**
2♠	dbl	pass	?

♠ J 6 4
♥ A K 8 6
♦ 7 2
♣ Q 7 6 4

With nine working points, you have enough to bid a direct 3♥ — invitational and non-forcing.

W	N	E	S
2♠	dbl	pass	?

♠ A Q J
♥ A 8
♦ 8 4 3 2
♣ 7 6 4 2

This would be an ideal natural 2NT but that bid has been traded in. One option is to try 3NT and hope for the best. Another is to sit for the double. A third is to bid 2NT and play in 3♣ or 3♦, both of which could be either the right contract or totally ridiculous. Considering the options, on the near certain assumption that the ♠K is off-side, you have three certain tricks, requiring six from partner to make 3NT. If he can oblige, 2♠ doubled is likely to go for an enormous penalty and, at any vulnerability, I would prefer to pass the double. I have three certain defensive tricks and only three more are required from partner for a plus score. You should rule out trying to play in three of a minor and opt to defend.

W	N	E	S
2♠	dbl	pass	?

♠ 6 4
♥ J 8 6
♦ 6 4
♣ A K Q J 3 2

On this hand you have a source of tricks —clubs — so it's likely you can make 3NT if partner can stop spades. Although the double suggests shortness in the suit, partner is not prohibited from holding something like ♠Kx. The way to find out is to cuebid 3♠ — primarily, this asks for a notrump stopper. If partner cannot oblige, he is expected to bid naturally; if he bids 4♥, you can either pass or correct to clubs.

W	N	E	S
2♠	dbl	pass	?

♠ J 6 4
♥ A K Q 8 6 2
♦ 7 2
♣ Q 7

There is no problem here you have a straightforward 4♥ bid. There is no need to mess around with anything else.

W	N	E	S
2♠	dbl	pass	?

♠ A 8
♥ A K Q J 8 5
♦ 8 3 2
♣ Q 4

Now you are too good for a simple 4♥, although you can bid it 'in a loud voice' by cuebidding 3♠ first and then correcting to 4♥. However, an even better method (although I am not sure whether anyone uses this) is to bid 2NT and then jump to 4♥ over the mandatory 3♣. This should be invitational to a slam.

Lebensohl, like many relay conventions, is capable of an enormous amount of extension and complexity. Here's one further refinement.

W	N	E	S
2♥	dbl	pass	?

♠ 10 8
♥ K Q
♦ Q J 10 9 6 5
♣ A 3 2

You'd like to play 3NT if partner can help out in hearts a little, but invite game in diamonds if he can't; Lebensohl helps you to do exactly this, through the use of a 'contradictory' sequence. First you bid 2NT (initially implying weakness) and then you cuebid 3♥ over partner's 3♣, asking for some help in hearts, typically a half-stopper like ♥ J x x. If partner cannot oblige, he will bid a suit of his own and you can correct to 4♦, which he is at liberty to raise. If you had a hand of this strength with no interest in notrump, you could bid 4♦ immediately, very encouraging but non-forcing. An immediate cuebid of 3♥ followed by 4♦ would be game-forcing.

Points to remember

1. After a takeout double of weak two bid, there is less room available for accurate responses. Using Lebensohl helps responder distinguish among various types of hands: weak, strong, and invitational.

8

Facing the axe

Our next topic, which is likely to make for some very chilling reading, is the penalty double. There is very little written material available on how to handle the penalty double — and even the very best players have their disasters in these auctions!

Wielding the axe

Firstly, when should you double for penalties and when should you not? There seems to be a lamentable ignorance throughout the bridge world on this. A few basic rules are worth laying out:

1) If the final contract has been freely bid and the bidding sequence indicates that one or both partners are unlimited in strength, it is usually unwise to double.

2) If the final contract has been bid after a limited invitation and it is clear that both partners are limited, then it is probably right to double if *both* the following are true:

    i) You have an unpleasant surprise for them, usually in trumps.
    ii) Your double will not warn declarer so that he will adopt a successful line of play that he would not otherwise have chosen.

3) If, by doubling, you can indicate a crucial lead which will represent the difference between success and failure, then you are not only gaining the extra penalty but the entire value of the contract. Against this potential gain, you risk losing relatively little extra (unless they redouble!).

4) At matchpoints, when it seems clear that you are getting a poor result if the opponents make the contract they have bid, then doubling them can probably only gain since, in terms of the scoring, there is little to lose. The most common situation, in which many players 'chicken out', is the case where the opponents are vulnerable in a partscore battle. One down undoubled will give you +100, almost certainly a poor result if your partscore (2♥ or higher) was making. Double them, however, and you get +200, beating all partscores. At this form of scoring it can even be worth doubling them into game.

5) It is important to double in certain competitive auctions to warn partner not to compete further.

6) At teams or rubber bridge, doubling only gives significant profits when the contract is going down two tricks or more.

7) When you double, be sure that opponents cannot escape to a better contract.

So the first tip is this:

Take full account of every aspect of the auction

Let's, as usual, see how this works in practice. In each case, you are playing a team game. Think about your bid each time before you look at the discussion.

W	N	E	S
		pass	pass
1♦	pass	1♠	pass
1NT	pass	2NT	pass
3NT	pass	pass	?

♠ K Q 10 6
♥ 8 6 4
♦ 8 5
♣ 10 9 6 4

This came up in a teams' tournament and, sitting South, I argued as follows: West is limited to fourteen points and East passed originally, limiting himself to eleven. With the spades likely to be very badly placed for them and possibly other suits as well, I threw in a double. It turned out they could make no more than seven tricks in notrump. Actually, they ran to 4♠ and could still make no more than eight tricks. 300 for the good guys — the double gained 200 and five IMPs when our teammates were allowed to play undoubled.

W	N	E	S
1♣	pass	1♥	pass
2♣	pass	2♠	pass
2NT	pass	3NT	?

♠ 9 8 3
♥ A K J 9
♦ J 10 3 2
♣ 10 4

This hand came up in a 'top-class' team-of-four match, and is an interesting counterpoint to the previous example. At both tables, South doubled to attract a heart lead totally wrong in my opinion on at least two counts. Firstly, although West was clearly limited by his 2♣ bid, East was not (Rule 1). Secondly, even on a heart lead, it would probably be necessary to get partner in again to lead a second round, giving East the likely ♥Q and ♥10. There was no guarantee of this. Finally, there is no better illustration of how wrong the double was than the fact that the card partner actually led was the dream ♥10. That gave the defenders four immediate tricks but they could find no more, the full deal being:

North
♠ Q J 7 5 4
♥ 10 6
♦ K 9 7 5
♣ 9 7

West
♠ K 2
♥ 4
♦ A Q 6 4
♣ K 8 6 5 3 2

East
♠ A 10 6
♥ Q 8 7 5 3 2
♦ 8
♣ A Q J

South
♠ 9 8 3
♥ A K J 9
♦ J 10 3 2
♣ 10 4

At one table, East redoubled, picking up an extra 250 and six more IMPs.

W	N	E	S
1♠	pass	2NT[1]	pass
4♠	pass	pass	?

1. 4-card limit raise

♠ A Q 10 8
♥ 9 7 5
♦ 8 5 3
♣ J 6 4

Here much depends on who holds the various outstanding trump honors but again, while East is limited, West is not and, given your broken trump holding, a double may well help the opposition. These are two good reasons to remain silent.

W	N	E	S
1♠	pass	2NT[1]	pass
4♠	pass	pass	?

1. 4-cd limit raise

♠ K Q J 9
♥ 9 7 5
♦ 8 5 3
♣ J 6 4

This is a different matter. Although you have only seven points in your hand, you have at least two and probably three defensive tricks and this contract could easily be going three or more down. This time you should double — you will gain significantly far more often than not.

W	N	E	S
			1♣
4♥	4♠	5♥	?

♠ 10 8
♥ K 7
♦ A 10 5 3
♣ K Q J 5 3

This was another hand from an expert-level game. Although North-South were vulnerable and their opponents were not, South doubled and his partner respected this decision. The result was a big disappointment when the whole hand turned out to be as shown below:

North
♠ A K Q J 9 7 4 3
♥ —
♦ 9 8 6 2
♣ 7

West
♠ —
♥ A J 9 5 4 3 2
♦ J 7 4
♣ A 10 9

East
♠ 6 5 2
♥ Q 10 8 6
♦ K Q
♣ 8 6 4 2

South
♠ 10 8
♥ K 7
♦ A 10 5 3
♣ K Q J 5 3

Now, in fairness, a club lead defeats the contract but North led a top spade, after which there was no reprieve. West ruffed and led a diamond to the ♦Q and ♦A. The ♣K was returned and West won. He crossed to the ♦K, ran the ♥Q, ruffed a spade and drew the remaining trump. Now came the ♦J, discarding a club, followed by a heart to dummy and another spade, discarding a club. North was now endplayed.

It could, of course, be argued that North should not sit for the double; 5♠ is cold, even on a diamond lead. In my opinion though, the fault lay with South, the crucial point being the length of his spades. We saw earlier that a doubleton should not be treated as a shortness and this particularly applies opposite an announced long suit. South is not in possession of all the facts and should pass 5♥, leaving the decision to partner. In an extreme case where North is 8-0-1-4, it could well be that 6♠ is cold.

W	**N**	**E**	**S**
		1♦	pass
1♥	pass	2♣	pass
3NT	pass	pass	?

♠ 9 3 2
♥ A 8
♦ Q 8 3
♣ A J 10 9 2

In this kind of situation where dummy has bid two suits, a double of 3NT asks for the lead of the *first* bid suit, in this case diamonds. When South doubled, North duly led one, presenting declarer with the contract when a two-trick defeat was available on a club lead. In my view, South should have overcalled 2♣ when he had the chance. The suit is perfectly respectable and he was not vulnerable. The hand was:

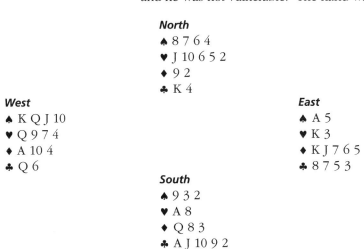

North
♠ 8 7 6 4
♥ J 10 6 5 2
♦ 9 2
♣ K 4

West
♠ K Q J 10
♥ Q 9 7 4
♦ A 10 4
♣ Q 6

East
♠ A 5
♥ K 3
♦ K J 7 6 5
♣ 8 7 5 3

South
♠ 9 3 2
♥ A 8
♦ Q 8 3
♣ A J 10 9 2

Perhaps the 2♣ overcall would have kept the opponents out of the notrump game, but it is better to concede a partscore than to risk their making a doubled game!

W	N	E	S
1♦	pass	1♥	pass
1♠	pass	1NT	pass
2NT	pass	3NT	?

♠ 9 6 4
♥ A J 7 5
♦ 8
♣ 10 9 8 6 4

I held this hand in a teams' tournament. In this situation, it was obvious that both opponents were limited and that the red suits, at least, were probably lying badly for them. Therefore I doubled, and this worked out sensationally when the full deal was as shown below:

North
♠ K 7 3
♥ K 4
♦ 9 6 5 4 2
♣ A J 3

West
♠ A J 8 5
♥ 9 2
♦ A K J 10 3
♣ K 5

East
♠ Q 10 2
♥ Q 10 8 6 3
♦ Q 7
♣ Q 7 2

South
♠ 9 6 4
♥ A J 7 5
♦ 8
♣ 10 9 8 6 4

On the ♣10 lead, East called for the ♣K from dummy and won the third round. Crediting me with 'points' for my double, he tried the spade finesse and finished up four down for -800.

W	N	E	S
		1NT	pass
2♣	pass	2♠	pass
3♠¹	pass	4♠	?

1. Invitational

♠ 3
♥ K Q J 9
♦ J 10 9 5
♣ Q J 10 4

I picked up this hand in a pairs' contest and again noted that both opponents were limited. A 4-1 trump split seemed certain so, with no tenaces, I doubled. Declarer played me for the trump stack and finished up two down when he might have got out for only one. That was +500 for an outright top.

W	N	E	S
1♠	pass	2♦	3♣
pass	4♣	5♣[1]	pass
6♠[2]	pass	pass	dbl[3]
pass	7♣	pass[4]	pass
7♠[5]	pass	pass	?

1. Invitational
2. After a very long pause
3. Promises one trick
4. First-round club control
5. Even longer pause

With East-West vulnerable, playing teams, South's hand on the auction shown to the left was the following:

♠ 7 2   ♥ A 7 5   ♦ 5 3   ♣ A K J 9 6 4

This is a hand that I had originally presented as an opening lead problem in one of my play/defense books! With thirty IMPs at stake, it is worth another look. Again, a double asks for the lead of dummy's first bid suit and I therefore passed, hoping for a heart lead. Sadly, my partner led a trump and that was effectively the end of the match, the full deal being:

North
♠ 4 3
♥ J 9 6 2
♦ 10 8 4
♣ Q 10 8 5

West
♠ K Q 10 8 6 5
♥ K 4
♦ K 6
♣ 7 3 2

East
♠ A J 9
♥ Q 10 8 3
♦ A Q J 9 7 2
♣ —

South
♠ 7 2
♥ A 7 5
♦ 5 3
♣ A K J 9 6 4

Should partner have got it right? I think so. I'd announced one defensive trick, which obviously wasn't in clubs, and I hadn't doubled for a diamond lead. What's left except a heart?

Now, I'm not insisting that the action that turned out to be right on any of these hands will always work — I am not a results merchant and, in many cases, the players who took the 'wrong' decisions are markedly better-known players than I am. But no less a person than the late Terence Reese once wrote 'If they never make a doubled contract against you, you are not doubling enough.' Rather than being intended to hold up good players to ridicule, these examples are meant to illustrate how my approach to judging the prospects of each situation can be applied in real life.

Points to remember
1. Before making a penalty double, attempt to gauge the following:
   i) The general lie of the land — are cards well or badly placed for you?
   ii) The likely gain of the double against the loss if the contract is made — vulnerability and method of scoring will obviously be highly relevant.
   iii) The consequences of the double — whether the opponents can escape to a less dangerous spot, or whether your double might give away the position and allow declarer to make the hand.
2. Penalty doubles are likely to be wise when you have a very unpleasant surprise for the opponents, something of which they are ignorant. If a suit has bid against you and you hold AKQ, that is no surprise; the hand bidding the suit knew they were missing. But if you hold AQ10 or KJ9 well-placed over a bid, that is an unpleasant surprise. For all the opponents knew, those honors could have well placed for them.

To run or not to run — doubled notrump contracts

Let's take a look at an even more neglected subject - what to do when the opponents double you for penalties. Already in this chapter, we have seen countless points thrown to the wind, but they are a mere foretaste of what is to come.

We shall start by looking at notrump contracts, and eventually arrive at an important general principle. All these hands were played at the 1998 Macallan tournament, an annual world-class invitational pairs event with IMP scoring; each of the 1NT openers shows 15-17 points.

W	N	E	S
			1NT
dbl¹	pass	pass	?

1. One-suited hand, at least opening bid strength

♠ Q 3
♥ A K Q
♦ K 10 9 8 7
♣ 7 6 2

It is already playing with fire to be in a doubled notrump contract when you are open in one suit; with two (and having lied about your point count to boot) you are pouring oil on the flames! The South player sensibly removed himself to 2♦, eventually conceding a non-vulnerable game in 4♠ — just as well when it turned out that 1NT doubled, on perfect defense, would have gone seven down for -1700!

W	N	E	S
			1NT
dbl[1]	?		

1. One-suited hand,
   at least opening
   bid strength

♠ 9 4
♥ J 8 6 4 3
♦ J 4 3 2
♣ 10 4

This was the North hand on the same deal. Nobody commented on North's pass at the time but I would not even have thought of sitting for 1NT doubled on this hand. Those hearts are unlikely to be of any use unless they are trumps and the hand could be worth at least two tricks more in a heart contract. It is therefore surely worth going to the two-level. Luckily, South had his own five-card suit.

This pair had narrowly escaped a fate worse than death, but shortly afterwards, another pair wasn't so lucky:

W	N	E	S
			1NT
dbl[1]	pass	pass	?

1. Penalties

♠ A K Q 5 4
♥ 6 5 4
♦ J 4 3
♣ K Q

Did you agree with the opening bid or would you have preferred 1♠? Opening 1NT on this type of hand is a feature of modern bidding, many experts attaching more importance to describing the balanced nature of the hand and its point range than to showing a five-card major. On several counts, though, it can make little sense to open 1NT on this example. Firstly, this hand is hardly 'balanced' — it is hopelessly weighted towards the black suits. Secondly, if this is your hand and game is on, that game will probably be in either 4♠ or 3NT. In the latter case, you will surely want the lead to come round to partner rather than to these pathetic red-suit holdings (not to mention that the club holding is little to write home about!). Give partner ♦A10 doubleton or any heart tenace, and the choice of declarer could be critical. Furthermore, in this case, you do not want to play the hand yourself even in 1NT. Thirdly, if partner is weak and this is the opponents' hand, you have missed the opportunity to suggest what might be a vital spade lead. Fourthly, 1NT has little pre-emptive advantage over 1♠, only taking away the 1NT bid itself. Again, if opponents are strong enough for that, you could be in trouble.

Nevertheless, a world-class player elected to open 1NT with both sides vulnerable, and when he was doubled, he sat for it! No doubt, he was hoping for a low club lead (likely to be their longest suit), after which he could run five spade tricks and hope for one trick from partner — or, at worst concede -200 against a partscore for the opponents — a small loss. But this was the hand:

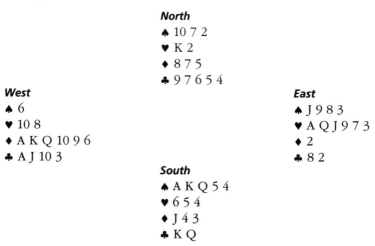

North
♠ 10 7 2
♥ K 2
♦ 8 7 5
♣ 9 7 6 5 4

West
♠ 6
♥ 10 8
♦ A K Q 10 9 6
♣ A J 10 3

East
♠ J 9 8 3
♥ A Q J 9 7 3
♦ 2
♣ 8 2

South
♠ A K Q 5 4
♥ 6 5 4
♦ J 4 3
♣ K Q

Six rounds of diamonds were followed by six rounds of hearts (East having plenty of opportunity to signal!) and the ♣A to complete a total rout and a thoroughly deserved -2000.

A number of footnotes are worthwhile. Firstly, note that even ta club lead would still have resulted in -800! Secondly, all the opponents are likely to make is 4♥, assuming they even bid it on a combined twenty-two-count and a minimal fit.   Thirdly, if we must play 1NT, note the considerable potential difference if North is declarer. Yes, it is the same on a minor-suit lead, but East has little reason to ignore his heart suit and now North-South actually make four tricks.   On a spade lead, it will be either three tricks or five depending on whether declarer can pluck up the courage to let the first spade run round to the ten — again a big difference.

Let us not neglect North's contribution, either. Again, it would not have occurred to me to pass with this hand. Even assuming the ♥K will score, the hand is worth only one trick unless clubs are trumps. In 1NT you are already doubled, but there is no guarantee that the opponents will choose to double 2♣. At worst, your hand should be worth a trick more in clubs, and you will break even.

So, after a long and patient wait, you see what I meant in my opening paragraphs in this chapter. This contract went for 2000 against 680 (assuming 4♥ making with two overtricks) — truly a disaster of titanic proportions, at least in bridge experience.

One would have thought that after that debacle, the entire universe would have been knowledgeable on how to handle these positions but no — scarcely an hour later, it happened yet again!

W	N	E	S
		1♠	1NT[1]
dbl	?		

1. 15-17 HCP

♠ 8 6 3
♥ 8 5 3
♦ 10 9 7 4 2
♣ A 5

With both sides vulnerable, what would you bid now as North?

As before, these diamonds are unlikely to be of use unless there are trumps but a world champion player sat for the double. This was the whole hand:

North
♠ 8 6 3
♥ 8 5 3
♦ 10 9 7 4 2
♣ A 5

West
♠ 7 2
♥ 9 2
♦ A 6 5 3
♣ Q J 7 4 3

East
♠ A J 10 5 4
♥ A J 10 4
♦ K 8
♣ 8 2

South
♠ K Q 9
♥ K Q 7 6
♦ Q J
♣ K 10 9 6

West got off to a generous start with a club lead but after that, accurate defense held declarer to six tricks for -200. Now, to be fair, 2♦, which surely would have been doubled, can be beaten by the double-dummy lead of the ace and another spade. The defenders can now arrange for ruffs in both majors to get the same 200. In practice, however, most experts would agree that a lead like that, sitting under a strong notrump, would be more likely to be the only one to give away the contract rather than to beat it and I feel sure that East would have preferred a club. After that there is no defense, and the score is +180 for an eight-IMP pickup on a low-level partscore hand.

The long-awaited general principle is surely now apparent:

**If you are doubled in one notrump and
have a five-card or longer suit, run!**

In my first two examples, the players showed an alarming lack of awareness of what was happening. A weak notrump is often doubled on general strength (in fact, many players get in trouble by doubling on too weak a hand, but that's another story). When a strong notrump is doubled, the doubler usually has a long running suit rather than just good values. This means that you can easily be heavily defeated even if you have a reasonable share of the points. The hand above, which cost 2000, was playing with a combined eighteen against twenty-two — hardly an overwhelming difference!

To run or not to run — doubled suit contracts

Many of the same general principles apply when you are doubled in a suit contract. It's folly to remove one doubled contract to another if you are likely to be booked for an even bigger penalty in your runout spot. But there's an other side to the coin. If you are satisfied that you are booked for a certain disaster in the current contract and there is some chance that an alternative could be markedly better while, at worst, it will result in a relatively small increase in the penalty, you should move. With this to guide you, try the next few hands. Each time, try to determine how clear-cut a decision it is to stay put or to run. In each case, you are South, at IMP scoring.

W	N	E	S
4♣	4♥	dbl	?

♠ 5 2
♥ —
♦ A J 10 8 7 4 2
♣ J 10 6 4

This hand game up in a World Championship match with North-South vulnerable, and South elected to pass. Was this showing admirable trust in partner or downright irresponsibility? Partner has bid under pressure and, when he bid 4♥, he was not aware of the situation. You are far more knowledgeable and your length in clubs, marking partner with a likely singleton at most, indicates that he is likely to have at least tolerance for your diamonds. There is surely no doubt that you should get out to

5♦. On this occasion, you would have hit the jackpot, the full hand proving to be:

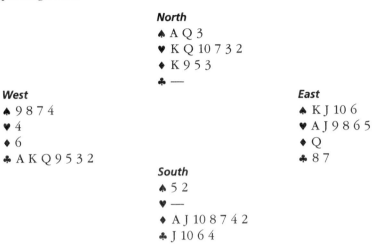

North
♠ A Q 3
♥ K Q 10 7 3 2
♦ K 9 5 3
♣ —

West
♠ 9 8 7 4
♥ 4
♦ 6
♣ A K Q 9 5 3 2

East
♠ K J 10 6
♥ A J 9 8 6 5
♦ Q
♣ 8 7

South
♠ 5 2
♥ —
♦ A J 10 8 7 4 2
♣ J 10 6 4

As the cards lie, a takeout double from North would have worked better but is that really right with such unequal major-suit holdings? I hardly think so. 4♥ doubled went for -800 and worse was to follow in the other room:

W	N	E	S
1♣	1♥	pass	2♦
3♣	4♣	4♠	5♦
pass	6♦	dbl	all pass

This contract was unbeatable so +1540 was added to the +800 already earned. In my view, as explained earlier, West was totally at fault. His hand has little or no defense and should be bid as a preempt or not at all. I would have tried a Gambling 3NT, but the 4♣ bid chosen at the first table is reasonable. As a matter of interest, a takeout double from North on *this* auction is probably preferable to overcalling 1♥ as there is room to bid hearts later. South's 2♦, particularly if it was considered forward-going, was certainly playing with fire but he found his partner with a dream hand.

W	N	E	S
1♠	2♥	pass	pass
dbl	pass	pass	?

♠ J 6 4
♥ —
♦ K Q 10 8 6 4 3
♣ 10 8 5

This hand was discussed by a world champion pair in a magazine article some years ago. This was their comment: 'Whether you should rescue is debatable. If the diamonds were a little better — say ♦KQJ9xxx — we would say yes; if they were worse, we would say no. Remember you won't get any thanks if you take out into 3♦ and go three down — even if 2♥ might also have been three down. Bear in mind always that, when you raise the level of bidding, you benefit only if you can take two more tricks than partner would have made. If, in the present example, you make seven tricks in diamonds when he would have made six in hearts, the result is the same — two down.'

As world champions, their views should be respected. But let's list a few facts:

1) In hearts you are definitely on a terrible misfit; in diamonds, you may or may not be — diamonds is surely the better bet.

2) The hearts are definitely heavily stacked against you, the diamonds may or may not be.

3) In hearts, you are definitely doubled; in diamonds, especially if partner has some sort of tolerance, there is no guarantee that the opponents will be keen to double. Even giving partner a small singleton, the opponents could have ♦Jx facing ♦Axx and no clear-cut double for either of them.

4) In diamonds, you have at least seven trumps between you; in hearts, partner could have only a five-card suit; he may have six, but is unlikely to have more than seven.

5) We now consider this business of two extra tricks. We need to compare how many tricks we have to offer if hearts are trumps. If partner has a diamond singleton or void, the answer is none! If he has two or more, we should certainly be playing in diamonds. Looking at the dark side, even facing a diamond void, a 3-3 split or many of the 4-2 breaks will give us five extra tricks. In the extreme case where there is a doubleton ♦J9, you have six extra tricks!

6) We have seen that you probably have no tricks to offer if hearts are trumps. This does not necessarily apply the other way. Partner could easily have ♥AK10xxx while the doubler holds ♥QJ98x — two tricks for your side, even with diamonds as trumps.

7) Finally, consider the cost of a mistake. At the very worst, if you run into a very stubborn partner who, with a diamond void and lots of hearts, returns to 3♥, your mistake will have cost 300. At the other extreme, by rescuing you might be converting -1100 into +110 or even +670. I know which mistake I would rather make — to me it is clear-cut that you should bid 3♦.

I would take a similar action (bidding 3♦), even with

♠ J 6 4 3   ♥ —   ♦ K Q 10 8 6 4   ♣ 10 8 5

for the reasons listed above, although admittedly the arguments now carry less force. Matters become more debatable, however, when you have something like the following:

♠ J 6 4   ♥ —   ♦ A K 8 6 4 3   ♣ 10 8 5

Now you have two certain tricks to offer even with hearts as trumps and there is no guarantee that partner has heart tricks with diamonds as trumps.

W	N	E	S
1♦	1♠	pass	pass
dbl	pass	pass	?

♠ 4
♥ Q 10 7 4
♦ 9 6 3 2
♣ 10 8 6 2

This was the next hand in the same article by those same world champions. Their comment this time was: 'Here you know that 1♠ doubled will be bad, so to rescue is right. You might try 1NT for the moment, intending to redouble when this is doubled.'

In the last example, there was a fabulous alternative trump suit to run to. However, here you are still raising the contract level, but there is no guarantee of anything better than a 4-3 fit and that could well be in diamonds facing a 5-1 trump split! Partner could, of course, have four clubs or four hearts but the lack of a takeout double makes hearts unlikely and partner could easily have six spades. Provided you are playing with a partner who will have a decent suit for an overcall, I rate it probably right to pass, with only a very dubious case for rescuing.

W	N	E	S
		1♦	2♣
pass	pass	dbl	pass
pass	2♠	dbl	?

♠ —
♥ A J 8 5
♦ 7 4 2
♣ K J 10 6 4 2

Here partner has taken charge of proceedings and, having bid your clubs, you have no right or reason to argue. Partner will probably have considerable length in spades to have taken this action and you had not promised any. A return to clubs (where partner clearly has no fit) or an SOS redouble, attempting to find a heart fit, is unlikely to achieve anything but an increased penalty and a very irate partner.

W	N	E	S
1♠	2NT¹	dbl	?

1. Minors

♠ J 10 7 5 4
♥ A K 10 9 3 2
♦ 5
♣ —

This problem was first posed in a magazine bidding panel and the majority of the experts voted to bid 3♥. Our world champions, commenting later, considered this 'debatable', expressing the view that, even giving partner a doubleton heart, 3♥ is likely to play badly and that to pass 2NT doubled is at least as good. If partner has a strong six-card minor suit, he can still rescue himself. Even if he has not, it should be possible to scramble a few tricks as the opponents cannot run a lot of tricks quickly.

This time I am with the world champions, favoring passing and rating the 3♥ bid as criminal. Two very important points should be made. Firstly, it is likely that both North and East are very short of spades: West could well have opened on no more than ♠AKQ9xx and a queen or jack outside and therefore might be terrified of defending. He might be tempted to bid 3♠ but certainly will not if you shout about the misfit at the top of your voice with an immediate 3♥. Secondly, by passing, you give your partner the option of sitting for 2NT doubled, redoubling for SOS, or bidding a six-card minor if he has one, in which case you have two tricks for him. After the redouble, you can always play in 3♥ if you still want to; little has been lost.

Points to remember

1. When you have been doubled and are considering running, think about whether you know something partner doesn't

2. How valuable will your hand be to partner in the doubled contract, and how useful will it be in an alternative one?

3. Don't remove one doubled contract to another if the runout is likely to be even worse.

4. However, if certain disaster looms in the current contract and the alternative is unlikely to much worse, and could be a lot better, run like a rabbit.

9

Bidding one more

Many readers will be familiar with the Law of Total Tricks, which was mentioned in an earlier chapter. For those who are not, we can briefly state it here: the total number of tricks available in a given hand is equal to the total number of trumps possessed by the two sides, each presumed to be playing in its best fit. Thus if you have a nine-card fit, and your opponents an eight-card fit, the Law says that the two sides can take a total of seventeen tricks between them. Notice that this doesn't tell you how many tricks each side can make, just the total available: it might be that they make 3♦ while the limit of the hand is 2♠ for you, or that you make 4♥ while they go four down in 5♣.

While the Law can be a useful yardstick, there is usually a great deal of other information available to help you judge when to bid on in a competitive situation. In this chapter, we are going to look at several recent examples where expert players have gone wrong.

There are a number of well-known tips that apply to competitive auctions, and again, many readers will be familiar with them. You've probably heard 'If in doubt bid one more,' and 'The five-level belongs to the opponents.' Unfortunately, to start with, these two obviously contradict each other — a great help!

My first piece of advice is largely aimed at the alarming number of players, including a string of well-known names, who might be described as 'vulnerability obsessives'. They believe that favorable vulnerability constitutes a license to bid on nothing while unfavorable vulnerability prevails as a strict order to show restraint on enormous hands. The tip is:

Look at the hand rather than at the vulnerability

Vulnerability is important in sacrifice situations when you are bidding a contract that you know you *cannot* make. Now the cost is relevant against the value of the opponents' contract — which you assume, often wrongly, that they *will* make. Few players realize that when you are bidding contracts that you think you will make, it works the other way! A non-vulnerable game, for example, is worth 300 against the vulnerable game worth 500. You should therefore be bidding aggressively when vulnerable as you are striving for a bigger prize. A missed game non-vulnerable will only cost you about six IMPs; vulnerable, however, it is ten IMPs.

Let's look at some examples. In all cases, you are South:

W	N	E	S
1♣	1♥	1♠	4♥
pass	pass	4♠	?

♠ 10 9 6
♥ Q J 8 4 2
♦ —
♣ Q 10 9 7 3

Playing IMPs, with E-W vulnerable, what do you bid now?

This hand illustrates an important point. There are three possible actions:
i) Decide immediately to compete further.
ii) Double, attempting to prevent partner from bidding further.
iii) Pass and leave the decision to partner, who may well be better informed.

Of these, (iii) is very often correct, yet far too many players take a decision when it is not their place to do so; this point was made earlier via an analogy about paupers giving financial advice to the rich. However, in the situation we have here, South should be decisive and in fact should have travanced the problem before bidding 4♥. He must either decide that his diamond void will provide sufficient defense to beat 4♠ and tell his partner so by doubling, particularly important after his 4♥ preempt has suggested poor or non-existent defensive prospects, or decide that he does not have enough defense and compete. The latter would be my recommended action: bid a lead-directing 5♦ so that partner knows what to do if opponents push on to 5♠.

This was the whole hand:

North
♠ A 5
♥ A K 10 6
♦ 9 8 7 4 2
♣ J 6

West
♠ K 2
♥ 9 5 3
♦ A 10 6 5
♣ A K 5 2

East
♠ Q J 8 7 4 3
♥ 7
♦ K Q J 3
♣ 8 4

South
♠ 10 9 6
♥ Q J 8 4 2
♦ —
♣ Q 10 9 7 3

As the cards lie, 4♠ can be beaten and indeed South found the lead of the ♥J which North should have read as 'something strange'. Sadly, North tried to cash another heart and that was that. But look at 5♥, which loses only a spade and two clubs for one down against a game which will probably make. There is no guarantee that even one round of hearts will stand up against 4♠. Also, South's ruff could well be partner's diamond winner anyway. Again, the little mistake (going down one when they were going down one) should be preferred at IMP scoring. In a situation like this, a useful tip is:

When partner is unlikely to be aware of the full facts, don't just sit there.

Take a decision on whether opponents' contract is going to make or not and then act accordingly. On this hand, South did indeed pass and North saw no reason to compete; although he should perhaps have figured out the defense, the absence of a double means that South must shoulder at least part of the blame.

W	N	E	S
	pass	1♥	pass
1♠	1NT¹	3♠	?

1. Minors

♠ J 9 3 2
♥ 2
♦ Q 9 8 7 4
♣ K Q 10

East-West are vulnerable at teams. What do you bid now?

This hand was reported from a teams event, and the writer commented that South 'had little interest in the proceedings.' South passed and the opponents bid to a grand slam in spades via a series of cue-bids, the full hand being:

North
♠ —
♥ 5 4 3
♦ K 10 5 3 2
♣ J 9 8 7 6

West
♠ K Q 8 7 4
♥ K 6
♦ J 6
♣ A 5 4 3

East
♠ A 10 6 5
♥ A Q J 10 9 8 7
♦ A
♣ 2

South
♠ J 9 3 2
♥ 2
♦ Q 9 8 7 4
♣ K Q 10

Declarer had no difficulty picking up the trumps on this auction, and the grand slam made easily. While North was heavily criticized for giving away the spade position, it is South's bidding, or lack of it, that I find impossible to forgive. Indeed, words completely fail me. It is surely obvious that partner is very short of spades and that North-South have a huge double fit. An immediate 6♣ (to ensure the correct lead), intending to correct to 6♦ when doubled, would put a lot of pressure on the opponents. But surely bidding to the five-level is the absolute minimum! As it is, 7♦ goes for 500, a good save even against game, never mind a grand slam. After the preempt, 7♠ is far more difficult to reach. It is more debatable whether North should have bid 1NT with such a weak hand but, on this occasion, he found his partner with a gold mine; South, to my mind, let him down badly and must take the blame.

W	N	E	S
	1♦		2♦[1]
dbl[2]	4♠	pass	pass
5♦	5♠	6♦	?

1. Majors
2. Values and ♦ tolerance

♠ A Q 10 9 5
♥ Q 6 4 3 2
♦ —
♣ 7 5 3

What do you bid now at IMPs, both vulnerable?

In the last example, I criticized South for failing to revalue his hand upwards following very encouraging bidding by both his partner and opponents. Now we see the converse — a player bidding his hand twice when not asked to do so. Once the hand has made a Michaels cuebid, it has said its piece and now any further action is up to partner. This is a classic travance position — twice! Here is the full hand:

North
♠ K 7 3 2
♥ J 10 9 8 7
♦ 7 3
♣ 9 4

West
♠ 6 4
♥ A 5
♦ Q 9 6 5
♣ A Q 8 6 2

East
♠ J 8
♥ K
♦ A K J 10 8 4 2
♣ K J 10

South
♠ A Q 10 9 5
♥ Q 6 4 3 2
♦ —
♣ 7 5 3

South bid 6♠, going for -800 when 6♦ was doomed. Of course, had the enemy spades been 3-1, there would have been no defense against 6♦ and an enormous profit from the sacrifice. There was no way that either North or South could know. It could be argued that East's failure to bid 5♦ over 4♠ is incredible, but that is his business. South was guilty of violating the travance principle. When North bid 4♠, he should already have decided what he was going to do against 5♦. And again, when he made his decision to bid 5♠, he should already have decided what he was going to do over 6♦. If he thought 6♦ was going to make, he should certainly have made no attempt to push his opponents into it! On this hand, South had no right to overrule his partner. He had his first bid — no more, no less — and, to my mind, he thoroughly deserved to lose the fourteen IMPs.

These last two examples combine to lead to a tip that is crucially important in competitive bidding.

Pay attention to partner's bidding and value your hand accordingly

Conversely, once you have bid your hand and have nothing further to add, assume partner has heard you the first time. Do not bid again unless either partner makes a forcing bid or it is clear that there is doubt and that he has left the final decision to you.

W	N	E	S
		1♣	1♥
pass	2♥	4♠	?

♠ 5 2
♥ A K Q 7 6
♦ Q J 10 6 5
♣ 10

What do you bid now at matchpoints, East-West vulnerable?

This was an example of lamentable lack of anticipation. With little or no defense, South elected to 'sacrifice' in 5♥ but he did not travance further competition from opponents. It is not only obvious that East has an enormous black two-suiter, surely eleven cards minimum, but also that any black honors in partner's hand will be badly placed. What guarantee is there that North-South can defeat a slam in either black suit? If you intend to compete over the game, have you decided that the slam will definitely go down? I suggest that North's opinion needs to be consulted and that, if South must compete, he should do so with 5♦; now North can decide the final action. This was the hand:

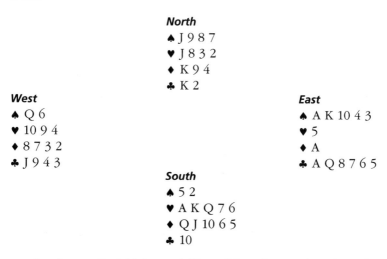

North
♠ J 9 8 7
♥ J 8 3 2
♦ K 9 4
♣ K 2

West
♠ Q 6
♥ 10 9 4
♦ 8 7 3 2
♣ J 9 4 3

East
♠ A K 10 4 3
♥ 5
♦ A
♣ A Q 8 7 6 5

South
♠ 5 2
♥ A K Q 7 6
♦ Q J 10 6 5
♣ 10

South actually bid 5♥ and West did well to realize that what little he had was worth its weight in gold and bid 6♣. North-South allowed this to play but could take the ♥A and no more.

Double dummy defense can defeat 6♥ four tricks for 800 but, in practice, it would surely only have been 500, the diamond ruff being well-nigh impossible to engineer.

My own inclination would be to pass 4♠, happy to concede 620 (or 600 on correction to 5♣). If the opponents do press on to slam, you can always decide to sacrifice then if you want to.

W	N	E	S
			1♥
pass	1NT	3♠	?

♠ —
♥ A K J 10 4 3
♦ K 7
♣ J 9 8 6 5

IMPs, East-West vulnerable; what do you bid now?

This is another example of a player failing to show a second suit when it would have cost nothing to do so. There seems to be a tendency in modern bidding to emphasize quality suits to the neglect of possibly good alternatives. Here, South squandered two chances — particularly unforgivable when his partner's first bid suggested that he might well have support for clubs. South actually bid 4♥ here and then persisted with 5♥ over 4♠ (breaking the other rule and bidding his hand twice!). This was the full hand:

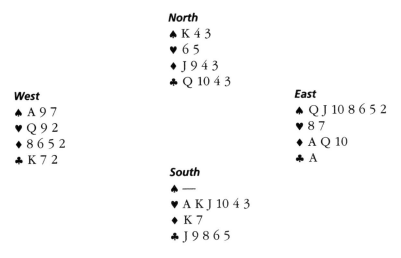

North
♠ K 4 3
♥ 6 5
♦ J 9 4 3
♣ Q 10 4 3

West
♠ A 9 7
♥ Q 9 2
♦ 8 6 5 2
♣ K 7 2

East
♠ Q J 10 8 6 5 2
♥ 8 7
♦ A Q 10
♣ A

South
♠ —
♥ A K J 10 4 3
♦ K 7
♣ J 9 8 6 5

Despite the seemingly favorable lead of the ♠A, South had to concede a trump, two clubs and a diamond for two down. Meanwhile 4♠ can be beaten by three rounds of hearts, North ruffing the third round low — the defense still comes to the ♠K and the ♦K. But look at 5♣: in this contract, South has no heart loser and at least the penalty is reduced to 100.

It is often worthwhile telling partner more about your hand in competitive situations when it is clear that both sides have a big fit and it is going to be a question of how high to go. Look at these two examples, neither side vulnerable at IMP scoring:

W	N	E	S
			1♠
2♥	2♠	3♥	?

♠ A Q J 8 6 5
♥ 7
♦ 8
♣ K Q J 6 4

W	N	E	S
			1♥
1♠	2♥	3♠	?

♠ 6 2
♥ A K J 7 5 3
♦ A Q J 5
♣ 8

The bidding may well rise to the five-level and, in each case, it is best to bid your second suit now and then allow partner to decide how high to go. If you jump to game immediately, you risk having the opponents compete and neither you nor your partner knowing what to do. The worst situation arises when partner doubles after some thought and now, if you bid again (arguing, not unreasonably, that your hand is very offensive rather than defensive), it may well be that the director will take a different view!

W	N	E	S
1♠	2♦	2♥	?

♠ A 9 6
♥ Q 8 5
♦ 7
♣ A K Q 8 6 4

This hand came up in a teams event many years ago and produced a totally ludicrous pair of results. Neither South could double for penalties, and after considerable thought, both elected to pass. When West rebid spades and East bid 3♥, both South's doubled, obviously for penalties now. I'm astounded that neither player decided to bid clubs nor notrump at any stage. This was the whole hand:

North
♠ 8 5 2
♥ —
♦ A K J 9 4 2
♣ J 9 3 2

West
♠ K Q J 4 3
♥ K 7
♦ Q 8 6 3
♣ 10 7

East
♠ 10 7
♥ A J 10 9 6 4 3 2
♦ 10 5
♣ 5

South
♠ A 9 6
♥ Q 8 5
♦ 7
♣ A K Q 8 6 4

Three rounds of diamonds, followed by two black aces, completed a one-trick defeat of 3♥ for +100, a disgusting result for North-South with 7♣ cold. The two South players showed a remarkable lack of awareness of what was going on. With fifteen points and all three other players showing reasonable hands, it should have been obvious that there was a great deal of distribution around. A simple 3♣ would have sufficed for a start, hardly likely to be passed out even if they were playing it as non-forcing. Alternatively, an immediate 3NT, intending to pass 4♥ (certainly a forcing pass as there is no way that the opponents are going to be allowed to play undoubled when North-South have bid a game to make) would have been reasonable. I sat North and would have bid 4♥ over 3♣ to show the heart void and a club fit, after which we might even have got to the grand slam (incidentally, swinging the match in our favor!). If partner had tried 3NT instead, and East's 4♥ had been passed round to me, I would have bid 5♣ (what has partner got for 3NT, after all?). This certainly would have got us to 6♣ at least.

We've just mentioned a very important concept in competitive auctions: the forcing pass. Just as you are well aware that bids can be forcing, in certain situations a pass is forcing — partner must bid on or double the opponents. It is hard to define every situation where a pass would be forcing, but basically it occurs when it is obvious that it is your hand. This is a very common type of forcing auction:

W	N	E	S
1♠	pass	3♠	pass
4♠	4NT	pass	5♣
pass	pass	?	

West's pass is forcing at any vulnerability: East must do something — either double them or bid 5♠. He is not allowed to pass.

In lower level competitive situations, the situation is often less clear. However, even when partner's pass may not be absolutely forcing, it's often right to do something.

W	N	E	S
1♥	1♠	2♥	2♠
3♥	pass	pass	?

Both sides are vulnerable: South can bid 3♠, pass, or double. He has to judge whether a) the cost of competing will be less than the value of opponents current contract (vulnerability comes into play here, of course), and b) the value of the contract if he bids one more is more than any penalty available from opponents' current contract.

Many players argue that the wrong decision taken in these cir-cumstances will almost invariably result in a zero or very poor match-point score, and I agree completely. However, what they miss is that if they pass, they are already booked for a bad result and their mis-take will therefore cost relatively few matchpoints. The potential gain by taking a decision one way or the other is far greater and therefore, at least in my experience, it is worthwhile sitting on one of the stools rather than falling between them.

Forcing passes also occur in slam-sacrifice situations and this will be a convenient point to introduce a convention that helps you decide whether to sacrifice or not. Consider situations where both sides have clearly found a fit and the opponents voluntarily bid a slam. The following auction will illustrate:

W	N	E	S
1♠	3♦	3♠	5♦
6♠	?		

East-West are vulnerable. At this point, as-suming that 7♦ will not go for more than 1400, East-West can employ the slam sac-rifice convention as follows. If North dou-bles now, he shows two defensive tricks and South is expected to pass. If North has at most one defensive trick, he passes:

W	N	E	S
1♠	3♦	3♠	5♦
6♠	pass	pass	?

Now South knows that his partner does not have two defensive tricks. If he has two himself, he passes allowing the contract to play, forgoing the extra fifty or hundred for the double. If he has none, he sacrifices in 7♦. If he has exactly one, he doubles and the decision now goes back to North:

W	N	E	S
1♠	3♦	3♠	5♦
6♠	pass	pass	dbl
pass	?		

In the knowledge that South has one de-fensive trick, North passes if he has one himself; otherwise he sacrifices in 7♦.

W	N	E	S
1♥	pass	pass	1♠
2♥	3♠	pass	?

♠ K Q 9 6 4 2
♥ 8 5 2
♦ A
♣ J 6 4

As I commented earlier, responding to over-calls generally is a minefield of errors. Once again, there are opportunities to share vital information with partner. Suppose you are South, both vulnerable, at IMP scor-ing; the bidding goes as shown on the left. What do you bid now?

Would it make any difference if North had bid 3♣ or 3♦?

Partner's hand actually was:

♠ A 8 5   ♥ 10 3   ♦ J 7 3   ♣ K Q 9 7 3

and 4♠ was lay-down. But over the 3♠ bid, you have little idea what to do to. Once partner bids 3♣, you know that your losers are covered and can bid the game with confidence.

Over 3♦, which he would bid with:

♠ A 8 5   ♥ 10 3   ♦ K Q 9 7 3   ♣ J 7 3

you know that there are likely to be too many losers and can sign off in 3♠. Note that either minor-suit bid in this situation must surely agree spades since partner is a passed hand. If the hand is short of spades, how can he bid now at the three-level when he could not overcall at the two-level at his first turn? A classic hand where you should take full opportunity to help partner.

W	N	E	S
1♥	dbl	2♥	2♠
3♦	3♠	4♥	?

♠ A J 9 2
♥ 2
♦ 6 5 3
♣ Q 8 7 5 2

Playing teams, both vulnerable, what do you bid now?

Assuming partner has a four-card spade suit, as can be reasonably expected, the decision in regards to competing further hangs on whether partner has some sort of club fit. This might well be the case after West's announcement of diamond length, so arguably you might try bidding 4♠ here. However, this is highly speculative and most experts would pass at this point.

If you decide to pass, West also passes and partner doubles. East passes and it is up to you again. What now?

When you passed, you chose to leave the decision to partner; whether that decision turns out to be right or wrong, if only for future partnership harmony, you should accept it. To bid again now is nothing but a double-cross. You are effectively saying that you are willing to defend 4♥ when it is undoubled but not when your partner assures you that it is going down by doubling — a clear case of insulting partner.

Thus, if you entrust partner with a decision, respect it, right or wrong. If you do not intend to respect it, take the decision yourself now, prepared to take the blame later.

Points to remember

It should be stressed that some of the biggest losses at the bridge table stem from ignoring this particular group of points.

1. Vulnerability is certainly important in competitive bidding when calculating potential gains and losses from bidding or doubling, but ensure that it is a servant rather than a master. The content of your hand is the prime consideration. Vulnerability is a factor in close decisions — no more!
2. With very distributional hands, aim to play rather than to defend.
3. With two-suiters, it is advisable to get both suits in to give partner maximum information. He may need it if he has to make the final decision on whether to defend, doubled or not, or to bid one more.
4. In situations where you know that a sacrifice will be cheap or that a particular line of defense will be needed to defeat an opponents' contract, do not just sit there — bid or double to make the position clear to your partner.
5. Where the hand is yours and you are not sure whether to accept the opponents' sacrifice or bid on, if partner has another chance to bid, a pass from you is forcing. The forcing pass tends to be more common at matchpoints where it is clear that you must double or bid on; this applies even in partscore battles.
6. Once you have bid your hand to the full, leave any further decision to partner unless he clearly has left the decision to you. Respect his decision once he has made it.

10

Hanging in the balance

Our last major topic will be balancing — bidding after the opponents have come to rest. Again, whole books have been written on this subject and there is no need for me to reiterate what they have said. Let me, as usual, content myself with trying to establish some general principles, while looking at the places where most players run into problems.

Firstly, you probably know that some experts recommend balancing on very weak hands, doubling after 1♣ has been passed round to you, for example, on:

♠ J 7 5 3   ♥ K Q 8 5   ♦ J 10 7 4   ♣ 9

Partner is expected to show restraint in these situations! Against that, they stress that you should beware of balancing, even on much stronger hands, if you are short in either or both major suits. For example, take this hand on the same auction:

♠ J 8   ♥ J 7   ♦ A J 9 7 5   ♣ K Q 7 3

Here, bidding 1♦ is merely giving the opener a second bite at the cherry. 1NT, usually showing 11-14 in the balancing seat, is certainly a more preemptive action than 1♦ but the hand may well be poor in playing strength if partner, as is likely, has the majors. It is certainly worth considering defending 1♣: this could be a big success if opponents are vulnerable and have a misfit.

Another important consideration is whether your points are working; you should be reluctant to balance, even if you have the right shape, with too many honors in the opponents' bid suit. My own view is that, if you habitually balance on very weak hands it puts too great a strain on partner. Remember opener's partner can have anything from 0-5 points a considerable range. One easy way to evaluate your hand is to 'transfer a king.' If, by adding a working king to your hand, you are good enough to make a takeout double when sitting over the opener, then do so in the balancing seat. After 1♥ with a hand like:

$$\spadesuit K 8 7 6 \quad \heartsuit 7 \quad \diamondsuit K 8 7 5 \quad \clubsuit Q 10 5 3$$

another king would make the hand just good enough for a takeout double when sitting over the bid. This is, then, a minimum double after 1♥ has been passed round to you. As a corollary, the partner of a balancer must deduct a king from his hand when responding, to allow for this.

Secondly, whereas a good suit is crucial for an immediate overcall (although standards seem to be dropping, even in this area, nowadays), you do not need a good suit to make a balancing overcall. Indeed, you may sometimes have to do it on a four-card suit (at the one-level but not at the two-level). Thus, after 1♦ has been passed round to you, there is little danger in balancing with 1♠ on:

$$\spadesuit Q 8 6 4 2 \quad \heartsuit K J 7 \quad \diamondsuit A J 7 3 \quad \clubsuit 7$$

or, after 1♥ has been passed round to you, on:

$$\spadesuit K Q 7 5 \quad \heartsuit J 10 9 5 \quad \diamondsuit A 9 7 5 \quad \clubsuit 7$$

Generally, however, the lower your point-count, the better your suit must be to justify bidding.

After a strong 1NT opening has been passed round to you, the popular approach is take the attitude that you are unlikely to be able to make a game. The idea behind balancing now is to buy the contract in a partscore or, at least, to get the opponents out of 1NT arguably important at matchpoint scoring. Again, some experts recommend balancing on one-suited hands as weak as:

$$\spadesuit K 8 7 6 5 3 \quad \heartsuit 8 6 \quad \diamondsuit 8 5 \quad \clubsuit 9 7 5$$

or on any two-suiter that can be accurately expressed with a systemic bid. At pairs a case can be made for this approach but remember that, opposite the notrump opening, opener's partner can have as much as a poor eight points and still pass — the balancer could be running into a big penalty.

Notwithstanding my comments in the last chapter, my view is that, in this area, vulnerability is very important. If the notrump bidder is vulnerable, even if you can make a partscore, it could still very easily be right to let him play 1NT, possibly picking up 200 undoubled — remember you have the additional advantage of the lead and it may therefore be easier than trying to make 2NT yourself. Again, I suggest that you evaluate your hand by adding a king and bidding on that basis.

When both opponents have been bidding, the first crucial consideration when you think about balancing is whether they have a fit or a misfit. If they have a fit, it increases the likelihood that you have one too. Also, they will be very wary of doubling you, especially at a low level, and you will usually be able to come in freely. But beware of the level. After the opponents have bid and raised a suit, it will usually be safe to contest at the same level in a higher-ranking suit but could be dangerous to contest at a higher level in a lower-ranking suit. Say the auction has been as shown here. It will

W	N	E	S
	1♥	pass	
2♥	pass	pass	?

be far safer to bid 2♠ than to balance with 3♣ or 3♦. Opener's partner could easily have a five-card minor suit and not be strong enough to bid it at the two-level, even playing a standard system, let alone two-over-over game forcing. If he had good spades, on the other hand, he almost certainly would have bid them at the one-level.

If the opponents have failed to find a fit, you run the risk of being heavily penalized if you contest the partscore — particularly expensive at teams' scoring. Yet it happens frequently. Three cases are relevant:

W	N	E	S
1♥	pass	1NT	pass
pass	dbl		

1) The opponents end up in notrump; in that case, you have to be very clear whether a balancing double is for takeout or penalties. Usually, if you pass over one of a suit and then double notrump, it indicates that you have the suit stacked. For example, here partner should have a decent opening bid and a heart suit on this auction (else why did he not compete in the first place?). You can bid or pass according to your hand.

W	N	E	S
		1♥	pass
1♠	pass	2♣	pass
2♥	pass	pass	?

2) Their bidding has died after what may be false preference. There may be no safe place for your side to play this hand.

W	N	E	S
1♥	pass	1NT	pass
2♥	pass	pass	?

3) A probable misfit exists after one or both opponents have rebid a suit. Again, balancing is a riskier proposition: East may be loaded with minors, and there's nothing preventing opener from holding a spade suit.

Let's look at some examples of balancing decisions. In each case, you are South.

W	N	E	S
1♣	pass	pass	?

♠ 4
♥ A Q 10 9 5 3
♦ A 10 8 5
♣ 9 4

East-West vulnerable, IMPs.
Even when it is 'obvious' to balance, it may not be right. 'No problem here!' I thought, as I balanced with 1♥. I had, of course, kept the bidding alive for opener rather than partner. The next thing I knew, I had conceded -650 in 4♠ rather than the -130 I could have settled for by leaving 1♣ in peace, West holding a massive black two-suiter. Even if partner has some points here, you may well be outgunned in spades anyway and it is wise to let sleeping dogs lie.

W	N	E	S
1♣	pass	pass	?

♠ Q 8 6 4
♥ Q 9 5 3
♦ J 10 8 5
♣ K

IMPs, both vulnerable.
What about this one? Your honors are scattered and of dubious value on offense, while the ♣K is probably worthless; it is wise to pass.

W	N	E	S
1♦	pass	pass	?

♠ Q 6 4
♥ 9 5
♦ K J 10 8 5
♣ A Q 8

Matchpoints, North-South vulnerable.
This looks like an obvious 1NT, but again it is probably better to pass. You are surely beating 1♦ comfortably — indeed, if opponents were vulnerable, a pass would be clear-cut. Yes, you could make 1NT but partner might also transfer to a poor heart suit, rendering this hand essentially useless.

W	N	E	S
		1♣	pass
2♣	pass	pass	?

♠ A J 6 4
♥ 9 5
♦ K J 10 5
♣ 9 5 3

Matchpoints, both vulnerable.
Here you can try 2♠ — less likely to run you into trouble than double which might result in partner's bidding hearts at too high a level. He is entitled to expect at least three hearts. Note that holding three small clubs is a plus — nothing wasted, and partner is likely to be short of the suit.

W	N	E	S
		1♣	pass
2♣	pass	pass	?

♠ K J 6
♥ Q 9 5
♦ K Q J
♣ 10 8 6 4

Matchpoints, both vulnerable.
Your four clubs almost certainly mark partner with a singleton or void in that suit. Unless you are unlucky enough to find him with a 4-4-4-1 hand, he will have a five-card suit somewhere and it is worth competing with a double, since all your points are working.

W	N	E	S
		1♦	pass
2♦	pass	pass	?

♠ J
♥ 10 9 8 7 5
♦ K 7 5
♣ K Q 10 8

Matchpoints, neither vulnerable.
Your partner is marked with a likely five-card spade suit, probably a poor one since he failed to overcall non-vulnerable. Thus some of his values are likely to be in hearts and/or clubs where you want them. With the opponents having found a fit and limited their hands, you are unlikely to run into trouble if you compete with 2♥.

W	N	E	S
		1♦	pass
2♦	pass	pass	?

♠ 8
♥ Q J 9 5
♦ 9 8 6
♣ A Q J 8 6

Matchpoints, both vulnerable.
Here the principle of safe suits applies; if you are going to compete, 2♥ is therefore preferable to 3♣ despite the superior length and quality of the minor suit. West does not have hearts, but may well have clubs.

W	N	E	S
1♦	pass	1♥	pass
2♥	pass	pass	?

♠ A J 6
♥ 10 9 5 2
♦ 8 6
♣ A 10 6 4

Matchpoints, neither vulnerable.

Here all your points are working and, although you would like to have four spades, it would be a pity not to compete with a double here. It will be very difficult for opponents to double your contract anyway, and if, in fact, one of them has length in spades, he might reasonably take the view that his partner is very short of the suit and compete to 3♥. You will have an unpleasant surprise in store.

W	N	E	S
1♣	pass	1♥	pass
2♥	pass	pass	?

♠ A J 10 6
♥ 10 9 5 2
♦ K J 6
♣ 6 4

Matchpoints, neither vulnerable.

A similar situation to the last example, but the subtle difference is that diamonds, a dangerous suit, is your three-bagger. You don't want to end up playing 3♦ on a 4-3 fit when East could have a whole pile of them. Therefore, if you are going to compete, 2♠ is preferable to a double.

W	N	E	S
		1♦	pass
1♠	pass	1NT	pass
2♦	pass	pass	?

♠ A Q 6
♥ J 10 9 2
♦ A J 6
♣ 10 6 4

IMPs, East-West vulnerable.

Here opener could easily have a four-card heart suit and have been unable to bid it. You have most of your points wasted in spades and diamonds, the ♠Q is unlikely to be useful, and you have far more defense than offense. This hand is a disaster. I vote for a pass — note that the favorable vulnerability is neither here nor there.

W	N	E	S
1♣	pass	1♠	pass
2♣	pass	pass	?

♠ Q J 10 9 8
♥ A 2
♦ A 8 6 4
♣ 6 4

Matchpoints, neither vulnerable.

When this hand came up, I stupidly passed as South and 2♣ was made when we were cold for nine tricks in spades. The spade suit is good enough to stand a misfit and/or a bad trump split and there is no guarantee that East has more than four small spades anyway.

W	N	E	S
1♣	pass	1♠	pass
2♣	pass	pass	?

♠ K 7 6 5 4 3
♥ K 2
♦ K J 4
♣ 6 4

Matchpoints, neither vulnerable.
This one is less clear, however. If you bid 2♠ now East may have quite a good spade suit; you could well be losing three or four tricks in the trump suit as against two on the last hand. Furthermore, your side-suit cards are probably badly placed. This time, 'pass' is the right action.

W	N	E	S
		1♣	pass
1NT	pass	2♥	pass
pass	?		

♠ A K
♥ 9 4 2
♦ K 10 9 4 2
♣ K J 4

Matchpoints, neither vulnerable.
Even with this strong a hand, it is rarely right to compete at the three-level in a minor as the 1NT bidder could easily have a trump stack. You made your decision on this one when you passed over 1♥; it hasn't become any safer to bid diamonds on a bad suit.

W	N	E	S
1♦	pass	1♥	pass
2♦	pass	1♥	pass
pass	dbl	pass	?

♠ Q 10 7 3
♥ K 5 4 3 2
♦ 4 2
♣ 9 4

IMPs, neither vulnerable.
It is tempting to pass the double with five trumps but East will probably have at least six and, with your spot cards so poor, the surprise may not hurt him. It is probably better to bid 2♠.

W	N	E	S
2♥¹	pass	pass	?

1. 6-10 pts, 6-
   card suit

♠ 10 7 6 5 3
♥ K 2
♦ K Q 2
♣ A 6 4

Matchpoints, neither vulnerable.
Yes, balancing here *could* result in a massive penalty but, particularly at matchpoints, it is worth bidding as you will lose out in the partscore zone most of the time if you don't. You should prefer 2♠ to a double as the latter would probably result in partner's playing in a 4-3 fit at the three-level and, worse still, the lead coming through your heart holding. Admittedly, the 'safe' and 'dangerous' suit rule applies with less force here as opener's partner could have almost anything and still pass with a heart misfit; but you still have to play a minor-suit contract one level higher than in spades.

W	N	E	S
2♠¹	pass	pass	?

1. 6-10 pts, 6-card suit

♠ K 7
♥ K 8 2
♦ K Q 7 6 2
♣ J 6 4

Matchpoints, neither vulnerable.
This hand is probably best passed since you're going to have to compete at the three-level. If partner has spade shortness, he certainly has a good enough hand to have taken action already. Meanwhile, anything you do could be very wrong. Bidding 3♦ could be disastrous while doubling could get you to 3♥ on a 4-3 fit (even if partner has four diamonds he's going to tend to bid hearts).

So far we have considered balancing after opponents have come to rest — they have bid their contract and you are in fourth chair after two passes. Sometimes, though, you will be expected to balance in advance — just before they are about to stop. The most common situation is the one shown here.   Of course, this is a much more dangerous position. You bid here because

W	N	E	S
1♠	pass	2♠	?

LHO may be intending to pass and it may be difficult for partner to balance if he has three or more spades (while you are short). On the other hand, opener may be intending to bid on — he could be just a point or two short of a 2♣ opener — so coming in now risks not only a crushing penalty but also placing important cards for declarer if they end up playing the hand.   Nonetheless, especially at pairs, there are times when you have to stick your neck out or risk losing the partscore battle; this is particularly important nowadays when it is the style of many partnerships to raise one of a major to two on next to nothing, purely as a preemptive measure.

W	N	E	S
1♥	pass	2♥	?

The auction on the left is a far safer one in which to balance with a double or 2♠ (even on a four-card suit).   One point working in your favor is that opponents have found a fit and will be reluctant to double you into game when the high cards in their trump suit may not stand up on defense. But against that, at pairs, they will often feel obliged to risk it. So, strangely enough, you will often be on safer ground at teams.

The most important considerations in your decision are likely to be as follows:

1) Your holding in the opponents' agreed suit.   As indicated earlier, doubletons or three small are likely to be the poorest holdings while with one or four, you can be confident of ruffing values and

minimal losses in that suit. Also, if you have honors in their suit, you are likely to be better off defending.

2) The texture of your suit (or suits if you are doubling for takeout or bidding unusual notrump for the minors). Here you are sitting under the strong hand so lonely kings and queens are unlikely to be pulling their weight. A further point here is that, if you do push your opponents up by competing, they might decide to bid an anti-percentage game which is actually making.

3) If you are thinking of balancing holding four small in the opponents suit, remember that partner has failed to make a takeout double despite having a singleton or void in their suit, so his point-count is likely to be fairly limited.

Try these example hands on this bidding sequence.

W	**N**	**E**	**S**
1♠	pass	2♠	?

Matchpoints, neither side vulnerable.

a) ♠ 7
    ♥ K 8 7 5
    ♦ K Q 6 3
    ♣ K Q 8 4

b) ♠ 7
    ♥ K 5 2
    ♦ A Q 8 4
    ♣ A J 8 3 2

c) ♠ K 8
    ♥ 9 7 5 4
    ♦ A K 8 4
    ♣ A Q 7

d) ♠ A
    ♥ A J 10 7
    ♦ A J 10 5
    ♣ 10 9 7 5

e) ♠ 7 3
    ♥ K Q 8 7 5
    ♦ K 6
    ♣ K 8 4 2

f) ♠ 7 6 5 2
    ♥ 2
    ♦ A K 8 4
    ♣ A K 8 3

g) ♠ K 8
    ♥ 9 7 5 4
    ♦ K Q J 4 3 2
    ♣ Q

h) ♠ 9
    ♥ J 10 7
    ♦ A K 10
    ♣ K J 9 8 7 5

a) This hand is aceless but all your points are in the suits you are bidding and you have support for all three suits. A double is in order.

b) This is less clear. It is again worth competing but debatable whether you should go for the unusual notrump, restricting partner to the minors, or make a double which, in this auction, should be primarily oriented to the other major. My inclination would be the unusual notrump, the odds being against partner turning up with five hearts. Even if he does, he may still have a four-card minor and something like a 3-5-4-1 shape. The fact that you will now be playing in 3♦ rather than 3♥ is a lesser consideration even at pairs: any plus will be a good score.

c) Now you have tenace positions in both black suits and they may well both be adversely placed. With sixteen points in your hand, partner will be very weak and a pass seems safest.

d) The ♠A, albeit in the wrong place, will still score and the opponents will find it difficult to double you for penalties when they are short of aces. Make a takeout double on this hand.

e) This is awkward in that a double is likely to attract a diamond bid from partner and if you now bid 3♥, he may feel obliged to correct to 4♣ — much too high. An immediate 3♥ bid might attract the best lead against a spade contract but is very dangerous. The ♦K may well be badly placed under the opener and a pass is definitely prudent.

f) Here partner will have at most one spade and although he is likely to have long hearts, he will probably have some sort of fit with you in one of the minors. Your top cards are all guaranteed to score and I would bid an unusual 2NT.

g) Bidding 3♦ will ensure a good lead against a spade contract, but your black-suit honors are going to fall easily and they may be making 4♠ on minimal values. A further point is that a 3♦ bid might enable them to revalue a diamond singleton and bid on to game — the last thing you want. Though you are unlikely to be hurt in 3♦, you should pass.

h) Here it is worth competing with 3♣ as you may well make it and the top diamonds constitute some defense against spades even if partner now finds the wrong lead. A disadvantage of bidding 3♣ is that the suit is poor and West may revalue the ♣AQ if he has them, bidding on to 4♠ when he would not have done so otherwise. It is a close decision, but you might take the view that partner only needs one of the two top heart honors for there to be two defensive tricks in that suit. If so, you can risk competing, since you are not afraid of defending 4♠.

Points to remember

1. Length and point-count in the opponents' suits are particularly important in deciding whether to balance.
2. You should be keen to balance in higher-ranking suits at a low level but more reluctant to do so on lower-ranking suits if it means raising the level; you are more likely to be doubled in a lower-ranking suit.
3. You can be more aggressive competing for partscores at teams than at matchpoints — the opponents will be more reluctant to double you into game.

In conclusion

Bidding is a topic about which I could go on almost interminably but by now, I hope, I have made my point. Much of this book has been spent pointing out what I consider the major sources of bidding error — conclusions drawn from my own bitter experience (no shortage there!) and from that of players of all standards from beginners to world champions. I have tried to illustrate how some of these disasters might have been avoided by straightforward and logical thinking and I have introduced a series of tips to help remind readers of the principles behind it all.

Some of what I have proposed is controversial or, at least, non-standard. While I hope that you will agree with some of my suggestions, you will, there is little doubt, disagree vehemently with others — and what a healthy situation! Surely, that is as it should be! However, I hope that you have, on balance, benefited from this book, and combined with what you have learned from the two others in the series, *Focus on Declarer Play* and *Focus on Defence*, that your overall standard of bridge and consequent enjoyment of the game (obviously the first priority) will have increased sufficiently to make it all worthwhile.